Becoming Yourself

Becoming Yourself

✦

The Journey from Head to Heart

Jan Engels-Smith

iUniverse, Inc.
New York Lincoln Shanghai

Becoming Yourself
The Journey from Head to Heart

iUniverse, Inc.

For information address:
iUniverse, Inc.
2021 Pine Lake Road, Suite 100
Lincoln, NE 68512
www.iuniverse.com

Cover design by Tracy Klas, graphic designer, tracyklas@msn.com

ISBN: 0-595-32474-6 (pbk)
ISBN: 0-595-66595-0 (cloth)

Printed in the United States of America

Dedicated: to the Spirits

Spirit Quest
Petroglyph in the Columbia River Gorge.
With respect for those who sought their own destiny
through a vision and connection with the spirit world.

If you wish to obtain information on soul retrievals, workshops, classes, ceremonies, or the various healing methods I employ, please contact me.

Jan Engels-Smith
LightSong Healing Center
LightSong School of Shamanic Studies
www.janengelssmith.com

Contents

Acknowledgments

As I think about the people who have influenced me with their wisdom, grace, and love, I am overwhelmed with joy. It is these people who, either directly or indirectly, helped me to create this material. Some are close friends; others I have developed an intimate connection with through their words and wisdom. Often I am asked what material I have studied, or how I developed the truths that I speak of. It is important to list these references and to credit those individuals.

Trudy Bragg, my hypnosis teacher. It was through her that I developed the practices of mind control, affirmation, visualization, mass consciousness, thought forms, concentration exercises, and goal boarding. Trudy is also a psychic and did a psychic reading for me just as I was ready to leave for Oregon. She told me that I was to meet a woman named Marilyn who would greatly influence my life. I met Marilyn McDonald on a kayaking trip the first weekend after our move from Texas to Oregon. Marilyn has taught, witnessed, and loved me through this major transition period of my life. Her generosity and brilliance has molded me and this book. During that same kayaking trip I met Barbara Scot, another outstanding woman who has mentored me with her wisdom, her writing, and her curiosity. It was on the kayaking trip that we put together our Nepal trip, which you will read about. Now mind you, I had known these women for only four days, and already we were planning a trip to the other side of the world! These two women are courageous and intelligent wisdom seekers. I love them both dearly.

Rita Kenny woke me to angels and angel guides and how to channel and receive information from other realms. She completely transformed my thinking and opened me to the incredible possibilities in life. Thank you Rita.

Sandy Ingerman, my most beloved teacher, brought the richness of shamanic studies, soul retrieval, and journey work into full multidimensional technicolor. I am who I am, and doing what I do, because of this magnificent teacher and friend. Michael Harner, creator of the Foundation for Shamanic Studies, I revere for his outstanding research and development of shamanism today. Michael has committed his life to his work so that we all can benefit.

Other teachers—Kay Whitaker, Buck GhostHorse, and the spirits of the Tarot—have enriched my life tremendously, opening my eyes and awakening my spirit.

I honor my personal friends who, through their love, patience, and willing presence, have allowed me to tell story after story, and to bounce ideas and concepts off of them. They have supported me through my changes and my growth. A special love and thanks go to (in first-name alphabetical order) Claudia Ringler, Dee Hasted, Inez Stockard, Jeanne Tyler, Jo Shird, Kathy Hoggatt, MaryEllen Churchill, Paul GhostHorse, and Virginia Hudson.

A special thanks, also goes to my students and clients. Even though I cannot list all of them individually, I want to honor them. As I have taught and counseled, I have learned. These people have enlightened my life, supported me, loved me, and encouraged me. It is through their reverence for me that I even considered writing this book.

The authors who have influenced me are: MaryAnn Williamson, Catherine Ponder, Shakti Gawain, Ted Andrews, Sandra Ingerman, Kay Whitaker, Michael Harner, the group that composed the Course in Miracles, and Donald Neal Walsh. I read the first *Conversations with God* book just as I was finishing my first draft of *Becoming Yourself*. I found myself saying, YES. I was so thrilled to think that "God" had some of the same ideas I did!

A special thanks goes to my family of origin: my mom(s), sister, and dad. It is through life and all that it offers that one comes into herself. I thank them for their support and love. Of course, the other major influence in my life is my extraordinary husband, Ed. It is because of him that I had the permission and encouragement to grow, question, and develop. He has brought to my life perfection. He has taught me about listening, speaking, and understanding from the heart. He is my greatest earthly teacher, my treasure, my beloved everything. Because of him and our three beautiful children my life is full and complete. I could never want for anything more.

Introduction

A sculptor was once asked how he created such marvelous results from the stone he worked. He replied, "If I want to carve an elephant in stone, I simply chip away all of the stone that does not look like an elephant."

The artist's creative process involved finding the inherent qualities of the stone and revealing them to the eye. The challenge is to find the truth within the medium.

The sculptor's statement is relevant to the process of self-realization as well. In our efforts to find ourselves, we often believe it necessary to reinvent or alter ourselves into someone entirely different from who we are. We overlook the inherent truth within ourselves. Becoming ourselves is the process of chipping away that which is not us and discovering the self that has always existed. Becoming who we are is finding the divine self—the work of exquisite art—the universe embedded in our soul. Becoming who we are—the true "us"—is a path to healing and enlightenment.

Finding ourselves, however, is not easily achieved. It requires letting go of previously held ideas, or "states of mind," and uncovering the wisdom available in our own heart. Western rational thought has emphasized the analytical examination of self through scientific and qualitative means. However, reaching an understanding of self through purely analytical means is as futile as if the artist were to create purely from analysis of form and not from the creative powers of heart and soul. The journey from head to heart results in the integration of the total self—mind, heart, and soul.

In this book, I will outline a set of basic truths and unifying principles that exist to guide your life. I will weave together concepts and methodologies, share stories, and give examples of how to apply these truths to your own growth and development. Your current belief systems might well be challenged and you will be asked to consider perspectives that may not be part of your current reality. Your willingness to see possibilities, your commitment to finding yourself, and your energy of effort will do much to make your journey successful.

A Quest for Understanding and Connection

My story is everybody's story. My journey is remarkable, as a spiritual journey always is, but it is an experience available to all people. I consider myself to be an average American with average problems but with a divine connection to Spirit. I love Spirit and I love life. I believe that one has everything to do with the other. But my life has not always been this way for me. I suffered a great deal in my youth, as is the case for many individuals, and have spent most of my adult life healing from things that happened to me as a child. In the process of my own healing, I became intrigued with the concept of healing. I studied life from the perspective of science, psychology, indigenous cultures, and spirituality.

Since 1984 I have been a licensed therapist, and during much of that time I have worked as a shamanic healer. I have a full, fascinating practice, which has opened many doors of awareness for me. Healing, woundedness, growth, and the enfoldment of the soul have intrigued me and propelled me on a journey of exploration and discovery. What is life all about? Why do people become so wounded? How do they heal? Why does it take so long for some to heal? Why aren't people happy? Why do so many focus on what happened in the past instead of what is happening in the present? What is the place of spirituality in all of this?

There are numerous books on psychology that give technical explanations to these questions; however, they have always left me unsatisfied. My mind understood the concepts, but my soul needed more. The biggest void in psychology seemed to be in understanding the nature of the soul—the spiritual connection to healing. Just as there is more to life than what meets the eye, there is more to healing than what traditional psychology explains or what the intellect understands.

It is through my own exploration of self that I came into contact with Spirit and the wonder of the spiritual realm. Through numerous alternative therapies, I experienced a profound healing of mind, body, and soul. I have had incredible spiritual experiences and now plainly see that Spirit has provided me with these experiences so I could better understand my purpose in life.

While working as both a licensed professional counselor and a shamanic healer, I have found that many people are eager to learn; they want to heal. The continual cycle of unhappiness takes its toll, moving people to look for a better way. They are tired of the pain and victimization, and they are interested in having more power in their lives. We have a society crying out for change and for spiritual connection. As we move into the new millennium, our culture reflects a climate of more openness to spiritual topics. Spiritual growth has never been easy, but we are in a good position for this growth now.

Awareness is evolving in numerous ways. I see emerging connections between old belief systems and new ideas. There are bridges between traditional psychology and ancient healing ceremonies; there are parallels between the new sciences and the teachings of indigenous cultures. Old beliefs, previously rejected by science as primitive and flawed, are now reflected in the new sciences.

Indigenous peoples understood that the physical and spiritual worlds were part of a vast web of life—interconnected, interdependent, and whole. They understood that the past, present, and future are interrelated and that time is illusory. They saw existence as a circle without end, whole and unfragmented. The ancient elders embodied wisdom, seeing simplicity in the apparent complexity of life. They saw beyond their daily lives to their place in the "bigger picture," the purpose of life.

Unlike our indigenous ancestors, the current world perceptions are mechanistic and highly fragmented. We have not been conscious of the interdependence of all things. Science has explained the world and humans in mechanical, objective terms, and has failed to understand the organic nature of all living systems. Since the advent of the Agricultural Age, humankind has come to see itself as dominant over and separate from nature. The physical body, intellect, emotions, and soul have been seen as separate and disconnected systems. The emerging era, however, reveals the illusory nature of such perceptions.

Several theories have evolved simultaneously that reflect a more integrated and interdependent view of the world. Quantum theory has evoked a new perception of a connected reality that differs dramatically from Newtonian mechanics, in which all things are independent and unrelated and function like machines. Complexity theory now describes existence as organic and self-organizing. It compels humankind to see itself as part of a constantly emerging order with a universal consciousness. Our understanding of the brain and the clear unity of intellect, emotion, and intuition have created a new understanding of the ways we come to know. The new organic biology, and our understanding of ecosystems, has redefined life forms as not independent entities but part of a universal oneness.

New thinking recognizes a higher consciousness that explains more fully how life functions, without defying scientific knowledge. Wisdom recognizes the importance of nonrational thought. Knowledge without wisdom is merely fact without understanding. Our new age is tapping into the vast reservoirs of wisdom available to all who will see. We are approaching a time when psychology and science need to change. Quantum physics is opening new realities in science, and the pioneers in psychology are using alternative methods to open new realities in psychology. Through my own personal use of alternative methods I not only understand healing, I *feel* healed.

I started my personal quest for understanding through science, which led me to psychology, which led to spirituality. I earned university degrees along the way, and have spent countless hours in workshops and seminars. My love for nature brought me to the study of science and ecology, my love for myself led me to psychology and the healing of my past, and my love for God led me to spirituality. Initially, my spiritual study seemed to move me away from my earlier scientific studies, but ultimately it brought me back full circle. I now understand science and nature from the wisdom of spirituality. The circle, the hoop, and the medicine wheel I have learned to love and honor, from indigenous teachings, has brought me back to the beginning. I now understand all of my studies to be one study—the art and science of universal consciousness. I no longer see the disciplines as separate, just as I no longer see myself as separate from anything or anyone else. My spirit teachers are as real as my traditional teachers. The wisdom of the spirits is as valid as all of the university courses I took.

The ideas I present in this book are alternative and were learned from my interactions with the spiritual realm. The spirits have been my greatest teachers and my most beloved friends. Some of the information came through the process of my own personal journeys, where I was put in what I would call spirit school. "Journey" is the term used to describe the altered state of consciousness obtained in the process of interacting with the spiritual realm. During this phase of my learning, the spirits fed me ideas so fast I had to use a tape recorder to keep up with the information. Other information came through working with clients during their soul retrievals (a shamanic form of healing, which I will explain in depth) and counseling sessions. I have blended this information with my understanding of science, energy, and psychology.

I provide personal experiences to illustrate my teachings, and I hope that you can add your own thoughts and experiences to personalize the information. As you read, please keep in mind that I endorse no particular way to do things; I merely propose methodologies that work. There are many ways to contact Spirit or God. The shamanic style of contacting spirits, healing, and being connected on a spiritual path works well for me and my numerous clients. I hold no claim to any of these concepts; I simply explain things the way I understand them to be true.

Connection is your birthright; it does not come from someone else. Loving Spirit and desiring a relationship with Spirit helps your connection grow and develop. After all, if you want to walk the spiritual path, then you need to be working with Spirit. Each person has as much access to the spiritual realm as any other person. All people are spirits in individual form, and all can connect to the spiritual realms at whatever level they choose.

I have found that walking the spiritual path takes willingness, dedication and love. I have to be willing to risk and try new things as they are presented to me; I have to be dedicated to advancing my skill level. Journeying is like any new skill; the more I practice the better I become.

I choose to be very connected to the spirits, and they have asked that I pass along my teachings. I do this with great humility and love. My whole intention is to be of service. Hopefully something in this book will add to your own quality of life.

The Basics

o o o o o o o o o o o o o o o o o o o o o o o o o o o o o o o

"Your vision will become clear when you look into your heart. Who looks outside, dreams. Who looks inside, awakes."

—Carl Jung

You are an incredible spirit of divine perfection, the same composition as God. Creator is an ocean and you are a drop of water in that ocean. You carry within you the exact components and properties of the entire ocean. You are made of God, in the reflection of God, and God is in you.

This does not mean that you are God (as a drop of water is not the ocean) or that God takes on a human form as a woman or man (as the ocean is not a drop of water). It means that your spirit, which is housed in your body, is part of a giant whole we refer to as Great Spirit. God has many names: Great Spirit, All That Is, Mother/Father, Great Mystery, Allah, and Lord. All are interchangeable. In fact, everything is made up of the same energy. All things—every tree, rock, grain of sand, gust of wind, drop of water, animal, insect, bird, planet, star—are expressions of the divine, and we are all interconnected in a divine and profound way.

The universe is unlimited, and, if you choose to explore it, you will awaken to a whole new way of knowing—a whole new way of being. Spirit is available to all people at equal levels; there is no "better than," or "more deserving." The choice to raise your consciousness means to broaden your awareness, open up to new possibilities, step out of your comfort zone, and allow information other than what you already "know."

The following basic truths are unifying principles I have learned in my work with the spirits. They present concepts about healing and working with energy. Throughout this book I cite case histories and suggest how you might apply them to your own life to enhance your process of healing and well-being. I guarantee that if you make them a part of your daily life, your life will change accordingly.

Anyone, at any time, can make choices for happiness and for healing. This includes *you*. Read the following truths and begin to ask how they might affect your life.

Universal Truths

1. God loves and values you unconditionally.

2. You are first and foremost a spirit—a soul having an earth experience. This earth-walk is but one fraction of your being.

3. Your spirit has a divine purpose.

4. You agreed to forget previous existence. This makes becoming enlightened a quality of *remembering* who you are. Remembering is embracing this reality and then making the necessary changes in your life to reflect this truth. Respect, honor, compassion, and reverence for all life are necessary components for the path to awareness.

5. You are here on earth to experience, to create with Creator, and to remember. If you do nothing more from this point on in your personal growth, you will achieve two out of the three before you die. You will *experience* and you will *create*. You cannot help it. It is happening every second of every day. It will, however, take a conscious decision to *remember*. It is a conscious decision to awaken, to grow spiritually, to become.

6. Walking the spiritual path means that *you* made a decision to seek the truth of who you are. The quality of life that you live is strictly a *matter of choice*. You may choose to live your life at any level of awareness; all are honored and respected; nothing is judged.

7. The universe is continually offering opportunities, opening doors, and answering prayers. You can *choose* to be conscious and awaken to these offerings.

8. Judgments, punishments, opinions of right and wrong or good and bad are human concepts. These concepts are illusions that hide the perfection of the soul. Judgments and punishments do not exist in the spirit world.

Life is the journey of becoming, a continual cycle of evolving from one lifetime to the next. What you do not achieve in this lifetime, you will achieve later. You choose the rate at which you evolve. To follow the spiritual path is a choice and a matter of readiness, but it offers phenomenal rewards. It is a completely personal experience; no two existences unfold in the same manner. As the spirits constantly remind me, everyone participating in the earth-walk will eventually come to complete consciousness. It is only a matter of when.

Our job as humans is to clear ourselves of the many judgments we hold toward others and ourselves. Judgments are what most often get in the way of personal growth. When a person directs judgments toward others, it usually indicates personal feelings of inadequacy, unworthiness, low self-esteem and lack of self-love. Judgments can cause fear, hatred, arrogance, war, greed, anger, blame, jealousy, pain, and loneliness—the psychological disorders of the human experience. They are often imprinted heavily and cloud the reality of one's own being, which creates tremendous fear. Judgments have nothing to do with truth or the perfection of the soul.

Spirit does not pressure you to change, because you are loved unconditionally for all of eternity. The urge for change is a pressure you feel from within—your own soul urging you to create a better life. Happiness, peace, deep joy, and a closer connection to Source are all available to you. Something has encouraged you to ask questions, to seek, to pick up spiritual material. If your life is not being lived from a place of fullness, love, spontaneity, passion, sensuality, and divine joy, then you probably need to make some changes in your life in order to attain these qualities.

The Awakening

I was introduced to alternative healing in a very alternative way. I had a vision. In my vision an old Indian woman approached me. When I asked who she was, she replied:

I am you,
I am your mother,
I am your sister,
I am your grandmother,
I am the Earth.

She had gray hair pulled back tightly in a bun, and her skin was wrinkled and weathered by life. She was wrapped in a wool blanket and smoking a pipe. She asked if I wanted to join in the sisterhood, but warned me that my life would be forever changed. I was doubtful, but kept hearing the word "trust" in the background. I nodded my head and spoke the word yes.

I remember being extremely nervous, but there was a peculiar kind of strength surrounding me and supporting me. We sat down and she handed me the pipe, and we smoked it together, passing it back and forth.

When we finished smoking the pipe, she spoke again. "Your guidance will be provided. Your medicine that you carry is North, Wisdom, Healing, and Love. Begin at this time and learn to understand the Ways."

Looking back on this experience, I see the meaning of the vision with clarity and understand fully the intent of the visitation, but at the time I was left perplexed and wondering. I had had no exposure to any indigenous teachings. I did not know what sisterhood meant. I did not know anything about the pipe ceremony; I did not even know that it was traditional for Indians to smoke pipes. My only exposure to this Native American ritual was from westerns on TV when some white person would come across a tribe of Indians and they would sit and smoke the peace pipe as a sign that they would try not to kill each other anymore. I had no idea what the word "medicine" meant except as some combination of chemical elements to take when you are sick. I was engulfed in the mystery of the vision, but confused as to its meaning. Why had I had a vision? What did it mean? What, if anything, was I supposed to do with these strange images that had invaded my consciousness? So many unanswered questions…

Even to start reading about the Ways presented a mystery. What were the Ways? Where would I find readings that would teach me the Ways? I was involved in psychology in a very traditional way; I knew no other way. I was active at the time in the Methodist Church. In fact, I was considering studying for a doctorate in theology and perhaps pursuing a ministry. This vision was not at all a part of my existing reality system; it left me completely baffled. However, my love for God was so great that I honored the experience. I reminded myself of the many stories in the Bible where visions had occurred with wondrous messages accompanying them. I believed that this vision had come to me for a purpose I did not yet understand; however, for me to fully honor this spiritual visit, I needed to seek greater understanding. Thus began my voyage of discovery. It would prove to alter my very existence, and it is a voyage I continue to this day. The wonder of it has proven to be in the journey itself, not in any final destination.

I am a person of commitment. I am dedicated in the pursuit of my goals and persistent about overcoming any obstacles. My tenacity has often helped me to reach success in spite of difficult objectives. I love to see the impossible become possible, and the unrealistic become real. I did not know where the new challenge of my vision would take me, but I was prepared by habit to pursue it to its conclusion.

I committed to joining the sisterhood, whatever that was. I had made a contract with the vision, and I would keep my commitment. I just had no idea what to do or where to start. I felt that I needed guidance, but there was no one in my network of friends with that kind of knowledge, and only one with whom I was comfortable even mentioning the experience. It took one year before I found anyone who could help me understand what it meant.

I had moved with my family from Dallas to Portland. This move created whole-sale changes in my life: a new job, new community, new church, and new friends. I did not know at the time, but I understand now, that this move was part of a major shift that would lead to a reordering of my life.

Shortly after the move, I was at the Oregon coast with my husband, who was attending a convention. He burst into our hotel room saying, "Jan, come down to the vendor displays with me and meet this person who has a booth with some very unusual books. I think you will be intrigued."

I followed him down and browsed through the various books. They addressed a wide range of spiritual matters, many from nontraditional perspectives. I do not remember the specific titles of the books, but I do remember feeling an uncontrollable urge to ask the sales woman if she knew anything about visions. She did not, but offered me the name of a woman who might help. I remember the excitement—the bolt of energy—that ran through me as she handed me a business card with the woman's name and phone number written on the back. I called immediately when I returned to Portland.

The woman referred to herself as a channel, and claimed that she connected with the client's guardian spirits, or angels, for guidance. She told me over the phone that she felt my own guardian spirits could help me understand my vision. I caught my breath. The whole concept of guardian spirits was completely foreign to me. I had been to psychics in the past, but I had never experienced anyone who claimed to channel. I had little idea what the word channel meant or what I had gotten myself into. Yet still I was curious and felt innately that this was the right choice. I drove to her house.

The woman took me to a small room, and after some preliminary information, she entered into a trance and started speaking to me in a strong and unusual accent. My mouth fell open. I was overwhelmed with the information I received, but equally awed by the feeling of love that emanated from the words. During the session my guardian spirits explained to me the different symbology that was used in my vision. They also suggested that I buy books about shamanism, healing, and soul retrieval. I was to learn of this ancient healing technique. Through the process of learning about shamanism, I would remember many things recorded in the cells of my being that had to do with my purpose in this lifetime.

My mind raced at the conclusion of the session. I had heard so much that was new to me, most of which I had little or no understanding. At this point in my life, reincarnation and the possibilities of other lifetimes existed only as a part of Eastern religions. Now, I was being told that I too had had previous lives, and that it was possible to remember them. All of this felt very odd to me, but at least I had received an explanation of my original vision and a suggestion of books that would help me understand more. The directive to read was a comfortable and acceptable assignment, so I immediately bought several of the recommended titles.

From that point on everything changed. Due to this shift in my awareness and my willingness to open to new possibilities, I became exposed to the people, training, and concepts that completely remolded my life and my profession. Each shift has been a step along the divine path of my development and my understanding of how we all can heal.

Since the original vision, I have had numerous additional spiritual experiences. I began to reorder my life, renew my thinking, and interlace my knowledge of psychology with elements of spirituality and actual teachings from the spiritual realm. As I integrated these experiences into my own consciousness, I became acutely aware that my experiences were not only for me but were also to be used as teachings for others. The teachings and experiences hold universal messages, or basic truths, that need to be shared.

As I observe clients moving through their personal journeys from head to heart, two main themes emerge again and again—the need for self-awareness and the need for redefining self. The first is a need for awareness of their own intrinsic worth. Spirit is continually providing evidence that God not only loves, but also values each being beyond all imagination. In the process of becoming yourself, you become open to this reality. The second need is for redefining self in terms of this unconditional love. It is often difficult for the mind to grasp the meaning of a love with no conditions, but the heart is capable. Unconditional love is not based on what you do, how hard you try, whether you are successful, or even if you are a "good" person. There is nothing you could do to not be loved. In the journey from the head to the heart, one comes to understand this type of love and apply it to self. When you truly understand the unconditional love from God, you move closer to being able to love yourself unconditionally. Your complete self-acceptance replaces prior doubts, disappointments, and regrets. All of life's "should have," "would have," and "could have" feelings dissipate in a newfound awareness of one's own immense worth in the eyes of God.

Through my own experiences—my own head-to-heart journey—I have found that healing and the restoration of one's wholeness can be complete. Answers to the questions of life's mysteries—what is life all about, why do people become so wounded, how do people heal, why does it take so long for some to heal, why aren't people happy, and why do so many people stay entrenched in the past instead of alive in the present moment—all can be answered. The beauty of the answers is that they bring wholeness, understanding, happiness, and new beginnings for the people who employ them. What I have learned on this divine path is that life is to be enjoyed, and being whole feels wonderful!

The next two stories are examples from my own heart's journey of how Spirit unfolded for me the realities of personal divinity and unconditional love.

Mount Everest

In 1992, I went to Nepal on a trekking adventure. Although the trip itself was exciting, I was more intrigued with the possibilities of spiritual enlightenment in this most spiritual place. Nepal, like Tibet, is known for its high level of spiritual connectedness. Upon my arrival, however, these dreams rapidly dissipated. This happened for a number of reasons. I was traveling with four other women and felt as if I were the only one who took the trip for spiritual enlightenment. Conversations about spiritual topics were difficult, and most of my thoughts probably seemed obscure and indistinct.

However, the real hardship was physical. I immediately found that the sheer ruggedness of survival took most of my energy. I realized that my all-encompassing spiritual attitudes, so present in my usual daily life, are facilitated by a comfortable American lifestyle. Living in the United States offers me the benefit of extra time and energy. With all of my basic needs met, I have much energy available for a committed spiritual life.

In Nepal, I was more concerned with basic needs: Could I manage the grueling terrain, where was my next meal coming from, what type of sleeping conditions would I have, would I be warm enough, would I make it across the next wobbly bridge, and would I experience breathing difficulties at higher altitudes? My focus changed from a grandiose spiritual high to survival. Life was presenting difficulties with which I had very little experience. I did keep one focus though, and that was that I wanted a close view of Mt. Everest.

Even though Mt. Everest is the highest peak on earth, it is sandwiched between other extremely high peaks, making its visibility difficult. There is only one vantage point from which to see Everest well, and that is from the top of Kala Patar, a peak close to Everest. From that point, Everest can be viewed in all of her splendor.

Climbing Kala Patar is a test of endurance. One's skill level does not need to be accomplished to attempt this climb; however, the rugged crag rock and the altitude of 19,500 feet puts much strain on the body. I had been training for months before this trip, running 8-12 miles a day just to make sure my endurance levels were high and my lungs strong. I always kept the destination of Kala Patar in mind, for I believed that it would be the highlight of my trip. We spent two weeks trekking and finally we were one day away from reaching Kala Patar.

The weather had been cloudy for several days. The few people we met who were descending the trail from Kala Patar were disappointed. There was zero visibility of Mt. Everest because of the massive cloud cover. Still, we maintained our enthusiasm and plodded ahead. I kept thinking—within 24 hours I will be there.

I slept restlessly the last night, knowing that we would have to make an early start. In order to make it to the top of Kala Patar and back down to camp, we needed to start about 3:30 a.m. We would start the climb with flashlights. I woke at 2:30 a.m. and tried to center myself. In my backpack I carried a book called the *Course in Miracles*, a spiritual text with a series of 365 lessons and meditations, one for each day of the year. I had been a dedicated student of this material, and was continuing my commitment even in Nepal. While I snuggled down in my sleeping bag with my flashlight, trying desperately to concentrate despite my excitement, I read the lesson for this particular day. The lesson was titled, "Step Aside and Let Me Lead the Way." The *me* in this sentence referred to God. I read diligently, trying to absorb the words and waiting for time to pass.

Finally, at 3:00 a.m. we got ready to go. We all were very quiet packing our packs, arranging our gear, and heading out. It was totally dark, as the clouds were preventing any moonlight or starlight from illuminating our way. We forged ahead, watching our step, and tripping at times on the uneven rock surface. At this altitude the landscape reminded me of moonscape. Nothing grew here, not even moss or lichen. All was barren gray rock. We were lucky there was no snow, but it was late March, and much of the heavy winter snow was gone. The air was so dry that the evaporation process was rapid.

By 5:00 a.m., the sky was beginning to lighten, making us more aware of the thickness of the cloud cover. By 5:30, our party stopped to talk. There was much discomfort. The air was thin, making breathing difficult; there were feelings of lightheadedness and headache. One woman experienced extreme nausea. Everyone, except for me, was hurting in some way. They decided it was wise to turn around. I stood mute as I listened to my friends make these decisions, my mind blank. They turned and began to walk back down.

I heard myself speak, "I am going on."

They all stopped and looked at me compassionately, understanding my desire to reach Kala Patar. I scanned their faces. Although they understood, they looked at me with disbelief. I know that my voice must have come from the pit of my soul, because no one argued with me; I had declared my intention with conviction. We, instead, discussed options for my continued journey and made a decision of how to split up the gear. I would take our *sherpa* guide with me. We also discussed where we would meet up again, for all of us were unsure just when that might be.

As I stood watching my travel companions walk away I thought, "Jan, you must be nuts!" I was standing in the middle of the Himalayan Mountains with a guide who spoke very little English; I was committing to a climb that would tax my body, just to see Mt. Everest, which was currently completely hidden by cloud cover; and we were facing the likelihood of a storm rolling in. Still I chose to continue.

My guide's name was Nima, and he was an experienced sherpa. Like most of the sherpas in Nepal, he was in outstanding physical condition and able to maintain incredible ascent speed regardless of rocky, uneven terrain or thin air. Needless to say, I could not possibly keep up with him. Once we started off, I kept yelling for him to slow down but he paid no heed to my request. It was probably a combination of his not understanding my English words and his impatience with me. I must have seemed extremely slow compared to his native travel companions. I often lost sight of him as he scampered ahead of me. Early in the climb I was fine; my destination was clear and I was determined to complete the climb. Even though there was no path, I knew what direction to go—up the mountain in front of me. I did not need Nima to show me the way. My need of him was more to curb the fear I felt in the pit of my stomach of being alone in such an isolated place. It now was a matter of endurance and sheer will.

There were two moments of near collapse for me, times when I thought I just could not go on. The first time this happened, I dropped to my knees, put my head down on the ground, and tried to clear my mind. I happened to look at my watch and noticed the date. It was March 24th, my sister's birthday. I knew it was close to the end of March, but I had not been conscious of the date for several days. The thought of my sister's birthday gave me incentive to continue. The day became special, which transferred into energy for me. This newfound energy put me back on my quest.

Several hours later, I once again suffered near collapse and contemplated turning back. To my amazement, my shadow appeared in front of me. It was as though a spot light had illuminated my figure although the sun was nowhere to be found. I did not even know which direction I was headed. Yet still my shadow loomed ahead, up the mountain before me. As I watched this ghostly image of myself, my thoughts turned to my morning lesson in the *Course in Miracles*. "Step aside and let me lead the way."

At that point, I knew the will and determination I was experiencing was not me, but Spirit. God was behind all of this, pushing me, urging me, helping me. If I would simply concede to the climb wholeheartedly, it would be much easier. I was creating such difficulty because of my fears. I was worried about being alone, not being able to see Nima, about whether the weather would hold, or if I would be able to find my friends within the day. This worry was stealing my energy and blocking me from Spirit's incessant urging. I then understood the *Course in Miracles* lesson of stepping aside and letting Him lead the way. I let go of the control and mentally walked through the doors of opportunity. From that point on, I knew that I would make it to the top. Doubt vanished and new energy surged through me.

As I neared the top, the terrain became much steeper and the rocks and boulders further apart. I had to climb on all fours. I was concentrating on every movement. I heard Nima, who had undoubtedly been waiting for hours; call down to me from the top. "Look, clouds," he said, making a gesture with his hands to indicate that the clouds were moving apart. "Hurry, hurry," he motioned. I turned to look where he was pointing. Sure enough, the clouds were splitting like the parting of the Red Sea. Everest was exposed in all of her glory. He kept repeating, "Hurry, hurry." With tears starting to roll down my cheeks, I yelled back to Nima, "I see, I see, but I do not need to hurry, Nima. I think they are parting for me." I knew at that moment, that this particular event had been divinely intended. This is what the trip was all about. I was experiencing a miracle especially designed for me.

I pulled out my camera, capturing in a time-lapse sequence this spiritual event. As I completed my last few yards of the climb, my body felt disconnected from itself. I was overwhelmed with emotion, sobbing with such intensity that my entire body swayed from my laborious breathing and gasping for breath between sobs. Poor Nima must have thought I was truly losing it. He actually came over and patted my shoulder lovingly. It is unheard of for a Nepali man to do this, as it is a social taboo to touch women publicly. I know I looked distraught, and I am sure that I appeared to be experiencing a complete emotional breakdown. He was trying to help in a loving way that bridged our language barrier.

My eyes were fixed on Everest. I stared in disbelief. How could this be happening? Why? In the shadow of the world's tallest mountain, I sat down. I was overwhelmed, but still able to clear my head somewhat. Finally the tears stopped and my vision focused.

I noticed that a redbilled chough had landed about four feet from me. A redbilled chough is a bird that resembles a raven. It is large, black, and strong. The chough is striking in appearance with its massive black body and scarlet red bill. I kept glancing over at the bird, slightly aware of the oddity of its closeness, but would then float back to my blissful gaze of the magnificent Everest. It was several minutes before I questioned why the bird was at this altitude and was so close to me. There was no animal or plant life noticeable in any direction. Just rocks, glaciers, and mountain peaks—not at all the environment for a bird. In fact, the bird was the only other life form besides Nima and myself. I turned my head and focused intently on the bird. Everything became surreal. My head throbbed from the lack of oxygen, I was exhausted from the climb, and I was still stunned by the miracle of Everest's sudden and glorious appearance. I sat motionless watching the bird, so out of place in this bleak environment, and close enough to touch.

Finally, I said out loud, "What do you want? What do you need to say to me?"

I do not know the source of my questions. They seemed to emanate from some place deep within. Until that moment, I had never spoken a question directly to any animal, and certainly not with the expectation of communication. Yet some part of me, some cellular memory tucked away in my core, knew to ask and to expect an answer. The bird told me that I had been brought to this place by Spirit to help me understand my purpose and my worth. Much of the dialogue I had with this bird was extremely personal and I do not choose to divulge the details. However, the epiphany led me to dedicate myself to follow Spirit's call. After the bird finished speaking, he spread his massive wings and flew away.

I sat for a long time. I clutched my camera like it was my lifeline back to reality. I was glad that I had taken pictures of the parting clouds, as though I needed future reassurance of this miraculous and mystical event.

I was flooded with feelings about my family and friends. I contemplated my life and its meaning. I was consumed with love and insight, and I wanted desperately to reach out to my loved ones. I wanted to yell from the "top of the world" about how much I loved them and how grateful I was for their love. I was the recipient of a blessing beyond belief and I wanted to share this incredible love energy. The only way I knew to do this from my isolated location was to capture my feelings on paper. I decided I needed to write letters.

As I reached into my fanny pack to get a pen and paper, I came across a note. It was from my husband. "I am with you, I support you, I will love you always." I stared at the note in astonishment. I had rummaged through my pack a hundred times on this trip and had never seen that note. And suddenly it had made its presence known. My hand was trembling; tears rolled down my face. The words represented so much to me. They were the literal feelings expressed by my husband who lovingly supports and honors me, but they also represented a metaphor for Spirit in my life. I could hear God saying those words to me as easily as I could hear my husband's voice speaking them. "I am with you, I support you, I will love you always."

Here I was, sitting by myself in a country on the other side of the world from my home, having a personal viewing of the highest mountain on the planet Earth. I was being given direction concerning my worth and life's purpose. I was engulfed in a pure and wholistic love. How could I have ever felt unworthy in my life? I knew that Spirit was showing me my value. If it meant that I had to have a personal showing of the greatest mountain on Earth, that I needed to have a personal experience with a talking redbilled chough, and a personal message of love, then so be it. It was like God was saying, "Do you get it now, dear one?"

"Yes I do, I do."

God's love for me and for all of us is beyond human belief. I understood. This moment had been divinely planned to prove this love to me, so that no matter what obstacles I encountered in my daily life, I could refer back to this moment and remember. Remember the feelings, the awe, the immensity of this miraculous time.

At this point, I could absorb no more. I needed to move my thoughts out from me, to write, to ground myself by communicating back to the world I had known. I sat there writing, staring at Everest, shaking my head at the splendor. I was suddenly and completely aware of how outstanding my life was, and I knew it would continue to be so.

Finally the clouds started to come together, closing the window to my view. I gathered my things and knew I needed to start down Kala Patar. Nima was long gone. I had no idea which way to go; I just started descending. Down, down I went trying to find some sign of a path or a trail as I followed my intuition. I walked for hours and knew that darkness would soon overtake me. I remember looking at my feet, seeing them move, but not feeling them attached to my body. Something was carrying me along, moving me at a steady pace forward. The hours passed and I never saw anyone. Just at dark, I saw buildings in the distance. A familiar voice came out of nowhere yelling to me and to some shadowy figures too far away to see. I distinctly heard, "She's back, she's back." I had made it back to my friends.

Vision Quest

A vision quest is a Native American ceremony that in the Lakota language is called *hanblecha*, which means, "crying for a vision." It is a calling out to Spirit, to God, to Great Spirit with a request and questing for an answer. The vision quest is traditionally done for four days and four nights. The person on the quest sits isolated with no food or water and connects through prayer to Spirit. Different traditional cultures conduct the quest with variations in time and practice, but all share similar intents. In all cases, the person on the vision quest places himself/herself in a precarious position and trusts and calls out to Spirit in a ceremonial way. Additionally, other participants remain in camp and offer support to the persons on the quest. These supporters check in on "questers" periodically and pray for them during their vision quest.

It took one year to prepare for my hanblecha. Traditionally, there is a year of preparation, the actual vision quest, and then a year of unfolding. I am not going to go into all the details about my vision quest or the preparation that it took. I reference this story to underscore that God is continually teaching me about love. Unconditional love is the basis of the universe and spirituality. Too many humans have no experience of love without conditions, even in our most magical and intimate moments. In our society, love often has strings attached. Punishments, judgments, overpowering demands, and competition are all marionette strings that control human behavior. If you have not experienced unconditional love, it is almost impossible to understand or to hold its wisdom. I hardly have words to explain the phenomenon in general terms, and it is even more difficult to describe it in the way that I experienced it. I will leave you to come to your own understanding.

I had many mystical experiences during my vision quest, but I would like to focus on one in particular. I feel that this experience was not only meaningful for me but also contains a message for all beings. Let me preface the story with mention of a ritual that I did the morning before I left my house. I have a little bag of terra cotta hearts that I often give as gifts to my clients after I do a soul retrieval. Each heart has a word inscribed on its face to impart some sort of inspiration or message. I usually meditate with the bag in my lap or in my hands, asking the spirits which divine message I should give. I then reach in with my hand and pull a heart. On the morning of my quest I did this for myself. The heart message that I drew was "willingness." I took it to place on the altar I had created at my vision quest spot.

On the first night of my quest the moon was full. It was a warm August night. Nature had provided me with wonderful weather conditions and surrounding beauty. The moon was big, beautiful, and in full glory as I viewed her from my sacred spot. I held a prayer stick that I had made for the event—a sacred stick with white leather prayer bundles hanging from it. A prayer bundle is usually a cloth bundle that holds tobacco, which Native Americans view as sacred. Tobacco is often used as an offering to the spirits. If you place your prayer, through intention, into the tobacco, then wrap the tobacco up in a piece of cloth, it becomes a prayer bundle. I had chosen beautiful white leather for my bundles, and had treated the stick as a work of art for I had put much creativity and intention into creating this sacred item. In fact, my whole year of preparation had involved this level of intensity. I took the entire process extremely seriously and went the extra mile to insure that I prepared appropriately. I had no doubt in my mind that when I entered my sacred spot for my vision quest, Spirit knew I was serious. I did not know what would happen, but I did know I was there for a reason. The spirits had asked me to do this sacred ceremony in a previous shamanic journey, so here I was.

Even though I had gone through all of this preparation, there was one thing for which I was not prepared. I was ill when I began the quest. I had developed a severe sore throat and cold a couple days before the ceremony was to start. By the time I was to go to my spot, I was extremely ill. It took every bit of energy I could muster to go through with it. I also had no idea how uncomfortable I would be sitting on the ground with an aching body. My senses were dulled and whatever natural abilities I possessed were hampered by the oppressive aches and discomforts of the sickness. I felt very distant from Spirit. I found myself staring at the terra cotta heart "willingness." Even though I felt completely disconnected and discouraged, I had the willingness to continue and to trust Spirit.

It was about 2:00 a.m. and I was sitting with my back against a tree. I had been sitting for hours taking in the solitude of the night. It was during this quiet time that I distinctly heard someone say "Jan." I looked around, expecting to see that my support person had come to check on me. No one was there. I again heard my name, "Jan." I looked around again. This time I stood up and turned. I heard it a third time and realized that the sound was coming from above. I looked to the moon. Could the moon be calling my name? I was seized by emotion. My legs started to tremble, my eyes filled with tears. Because of my weakened condition, I had no energy to doubt or to second-guess what was happening. I just followed the direction of my heart. I raised my prayer stick to the moon and held it up and out, as if offering it to this mighty sacred one of the sky. I began crying out my prayers of intention. I knew that the moon was hearing me and communicating directly with me on this sacred night.

The next thing I knew I was traveling through space. I traveled up and up with the speed of light, all the way to the moon. I magically became the moon. As I merged with this great one, I could see myself standing down on Earth: This little person, holding her prayer stick into the sky, crying, and trembling both with emotion and weakness. Her heart filled with love, dedication, willingness; asking to be heard and noticed. I was overwhelmed with compassion, with unconditional love, with emotions that no words can describe. I had become the moon. I had become Great Spirit. I had become the universe. On an emotional, physical, mental, and spiritual level, I experienced a love that was greater than anything I had ever imagined—greater than anything I had humanly experienced. My cells throbbed as they absorbed and responded to this experience. I had no bodily connection to this little person I was watching below, but I had an overwhelming heart connection. I loved her beyond what I had ever experienced in the human realm. I understood what it means when God says to love unconditionally, not only others but oneself as well.

I do not know how long I spent on this sky adventure; I lost all track of time. When my spirit reentered my body it slammed me into the ground and I remember hitting my head hard. I also heard a thud, a sound like that of someone hitting you square on the chest with a flat hand. The experience was like none I had ever had. Even with all of the journeying I had done, I was not prepared for this encounter. The experience was not induced by drumming or intention. I physically and audibly heard my name called and I responded by making myself available. Spirit then took me on a journey to learn about love—the kind of love that Creator holds for us, and the love of which the universe is made. It awakened in me a deep understanding of what Spirit means when it refers to love. This love is of the magnitude contained in the light so often referred to in near-death experiences. It is the love on which enlightenment is based. It is beyond what many of us know, but it is within reach of all of us.

When unconditional love is revealed, it serves as an example of what life can be like here on earth. Spirit does not wave such promise in front of us and then say, "Sorry you cannot have any." Spirit allows us such remarkable experiences so that we can have a tangible event stored in our cellular memory to call upon when the time is right. This memory compels us to keep sight of what we strive for—peace, unconditional love, and freedom from judgment of others and of self. Spirit works in miraculous ways if you just provide the *willingness*.

Shamanic Healing and
Soul Retrieval

Learning about shamanic healing practices and soul retrieval became impera-
tive. Through the Foundation for Shamanic Studies, I contacted Sandra Ingerman, the author of *Soul Retrieval: Mending the Fragmented Self.* Sandra Ingerman
is responsible for bringing the concept, the training, and the healing potential of
soul retrieval to the American public. I strongly felt that I needed to have a soul
retrieval, and the information about journeying stimulated wisdom that already
resided in my soul. I remembered lifetimes of being a healer, and my knowledge
from previous lifetimes became available to me again. I not only reevaluated my
counseling practice, I reevaluated my understanding of the concepts of God,
Spirits, possibilities, other realities—the meaning of life!

Shamanism is an ancient healing art, dating back at least 40,000 years. It was
used by most indigenous cultures in the world. It is a healing method that
emphasizes that all experiences affect your soul and that all healing comes
through the soul. In shamanic cultures, the care of the soul is extremely important. In fact, it is the most important aspect of healing.[1] The shamanic belief is
that a human being is first and foremost a soul having a human experience, not
the other way around. If the soul is cared for properly, or is healed through the
process of soul retrieval, other healings can then manifest in the mental, emotional, and physical bodies of an individual person.

In our Western culture, we have doctors who specialize in everything imagin-
able except for the soul. To me, this care of the soul is the missing link in healing.
The soul must be cared for first. Fortunately, this is beginning to be understood
in our Western culture and more people are seeking out individuals such as shamans for their individual healing.

Shamanically speaking, all things are energy. The movement, or the transmu-
tation, of energy is part of the healing of the soul, which is itself, energy. In a
healing, the shaman moves out the energy that does not belong to a person and
refills him/her with the divine energy that is the essence of that person's true soul.
The theory behind soul retrieval is that there is soul loss when an individual expe-

riences powerful or traumatic situations. Ingerman states that, "whenever we experience trauma, a part of our vital essence separates from us in order to survive the experience by escaping the full impact of the pain" (*Soul Retrieval,* Ingerman, p. 11).

Through individual experiences, usually some sort of trauma, a person loses part of himself. In shamanic terms, this process is called "soul loss." In psychology, it is called "disassociation." Basically, it is a survival mechanism to withstand the pain of the situation. What psychology does not ask is where the lost part goes and how one gets it back. In the practice of shamanism, when a piece of the soul or energy leaves, it actually goes into another reality and is lost from the person. A void then exists in that person's soul. Think of the soul as a giant jigsaw puzzle. When you experience a trauma, a piece of the puzzle is lost, leaving an empty space in the puzzle. When this soul loss occurs, a soul retrieval is necessary to restore wholeness. In a process called journeying, a shaman is trained to enter an altered state of consciousness and travel into different realities to find and retrieve the lost soul parts. The shaman then literally blows these parts back into the client via the heart and the top of the head, restoring wholeness to the client.[2]

The voids created by soul loss can actually fill up with energy that is foreign to the soul. This can manifest into all kinds of diseases or physical, mental, or emotional problems. According to shamanic definition, the soul is perfect and divine, and life should reflect this. If a person is not experiencing happiness, or if there are physical, emotional, or mental problems apparent within a person, then evidence exists that there is not only soul loss but also an intruding negative energy. Extracting this negative energy and restoring the soul through the process of a soul retrieval thus promotes feelings of wholeness and happiness. One of the ways that indigenous people realized a soul retrieval was needed was when a person had stopped singing. With the restoration of the soul's wholeness, the person would sing again.

In a shamanic culture, care of the soul is part of daily existence. I believe that is why these cultures are notably contented, happy, and crime-free. People who are whole or feel good about themselves handle the ups and downs of life in a wholesome way. When people feel fearful, threatened, or fragmented, their responses to life are extremely different from those who feel trustful, optimistic, whole, and complete. In our culture, we have very little experience with sustaining trust and optimism. Our cultural system is based on a win-lose hierarchy. Someone is always gaining while another is losing. In shamanic cultures this win/lose phenomenon is seen as soul stealing, or stealing away someone's personal power.

Many people purposely steal personal power from others. A person can be the victim of this theft at any stage of life, but it often happens to children, especially if they are raised with authoritarian, controlling, or needy parents. The parents actually steal power away from their children. If a person is abused in any way, emotionally, physically, sexually, or mentally, there is a resultant exchange of power. The overpowered loses energy to the abuser. Children are easy targets to control and extremely vulnerable to soul stealing. The resultant soul loss leaves a void that is filled by negative energy (usually feelings of unworthiness) and the individual carries this energy for a lifetime, or until the lost soul parts can be retrieved.[3] If there is no care of the soul built into the culture's system, the result is a society of wounded people. Feelings of unworthiness can lead to all sorts of dysfunctional behaviors and attitudes that predominate in society. These feelings of lack can take generations to heal, but once the patterns are recognized efforts can be made toward healing. I have found in my own research that the core counseling issue for most people is the issue of unworthiness. People need to be genuinely loved and connected to a higher power. Once soul theft occurs, an effort must be made to recover it.

People also give away their power trying to find love or acceptance. Women have been taught to give away their personal power to the male gender. Cultural and family mores often create hierarchical gender structures, which establish male dominance. The result is socially reinforced losses of personal power for a false sense of social order. A country-western song like "Stand by Your Man" is an example of a gender-based system of control that suggests "appropriate" positions of power in relationships. Other examples of this belief system abound in our culture, but in true love and acceptance one does not give away one's soul. The void caused by engaging in this behavior can have extremely adverse effects.

Another form of soul loss happens in relationships built on codependency, in which one person bases his or her worth in another person rather than in self. "To rescue another person or to collude in abusive patterns is to give away one's soul in an attempt to hold onto the relationship" (*Soul Retrieval*, Ingerman, p.112). This is a false love that can create soul loss on both sides. True love augments the soul and is most present when the soul is whole.

Soul loss creates a fragmentation of one's wholeness. Consequently, a person continually tries to fill the voids caused by the fragmentation. Attempts at "fulfillment" may include overt behaviors associated with drugs, alcohol, sex, faulty relationships, or more subtle behaviors of verbal and nonverbal communication.[4]

Listen carefully to conversations. There is a definite exchange of energy occurring at all times. Questions about what you do for a living, how much money you make, what education you have, and where you live often establish a hierarchy of energy. There will be a winner and a loser in these conversations if the intention of the questions is to establish position. When positive energy flows, people recognize and pursue their interdependence. Interdependent behavior is evident in mutually supportive relationships in which individuals retain their personal power and self-worth. In such relationships, a person is not striving for worthiness from such external criteria as wealth or beauty, but rather from a powerful inner sense of worthiness. This worthiness creates wholeness.

It is important to understand that interdependence is not the same as dependence. In fact, soul loss is often the result of dependence. This is why children are so susceptible to theft of a soul part. However, many adults are also highly dependent on others and subject to resultant soul loss. The journey to restoration of the soul part requires the individual to first move from dependence to independence.

This movement from dependence to independence is accomplished by regaining one's individual power. Many confuse this transition with being selfish. They have been taught for so long to give away their personal power to meet the needs of others that this transition can feel jolting. However, the acquisition of independence allows one to participate in the universe in a positive and personally powerful way. Once one's independence is established, the individual is able to move from independence to interdependence, becoming a part of the wholeness of life without the loss of individual energy.

This movement from dependence to independence to interdependence is part of the larger universal shift to identifying with the web of life. The recognition that we are all part of one another enhances every individual's personal power. We are capable of ending our personal fragmentation and the unnatural fragmentation we have created in the universe. We can have wholeness of person and wholeness of life.

DEPENDENCE—> INDEPENDENCE—> INTERDEPENDENCE

In highly interdependent societies, where the interdependence is recognized and appreciated, soul retrieval is a daily and accepted activity. The care of the soul is the first priority in health, both for the individual and for the society. In shamanic cultures, a soul retrieval is performed within three days after any major event in a person's life. Traumatic or other dramatic changes, such as childbirth, marriage, death of a loved one, an accident, a broken relationship, an argument, to name a few, were addressed immediately by performing a soul retrieval. It was assumed that anyone going through such an event would have a high probability of soul loss, and in order to instill proper healing, the soul was attended to first.

Unfortunately, in our culture, years and years of fragmentation and soul loss can accumulate for an individual, which creates the potential for a soul to become critically fragmented. We can see the results of this by looking at the mental, emotional, and spiritual health of our society. We have a society that is depressed and self-medicating with illegal drugs, alcohol, and over-the-counter or pre-scribed medications. Our youths have difficulty finding purpose and meaning in their lives. Relationships and families fall apart with ever-increasing frequency. The culture is not grounded in taking care of the soul.

We are plagued in our culture with people hurting—physically, emotionally, mentally, and spiritually. The issues that doctors and psychologists deal with on a daily basis are what a shaman would see as warning signs of soul loss. Warning signs of soul loss can include:

- Anything chronic—fatigue, depression, misfortune, faulty relationships, emotional problems, suicidal tendencies.
- The inability to release some emotional trauma from the past—such as a death, divorce, or other loss.
- Addictions of any kind—alcohol, drugs, food
- Not feeling connected to the body or reality
- Operations or difficulty in recovering from surgery
- Repetitive sicknesses—colds, flu, and so forth
- Major illnesses
- No sense of direction
- Shame or feelings of guilt.
- Feelings of unworthiness
- Not feeling one's personal power[5]

Our culture suffers dramatically from these symptoms. It is rare to come across someone who responds and lives life from wholeness instead of from the woundedness of his or her past. If a person has voids from soul loss, these voids act like magnets trying to fill up with any energy to become whole. If you are exposed to anger, fear, greed, anxiety, unhappiness and hatred repeatedly, those are the qualities your own soul will absorb. Extracting negative energies, bringing back the lost soul energy, and then teaching a person how to stay whole will not only heal the individual and restore personal power; it will begin to restore wholeness in our society as well.

The positive shift many of us work to instill, in Western culture, is toward a restoration of wholeness and an understanding of our oneness. This work addresses the fact that we *are* energy, as is *everything*, and that all energies influence one another. We must learn to maintain and care for our own divine energy—our soul. In such a climate of responsibility and openness, shamanism would find a welcome home.

All of us have experienced trauma in some form just from experiencing life. Because of this, I believe that most people would benefit from an initial soul retrieval. I have witnessed amazing results in healing using this technique, and have also experienced it firsthand. Soul retrieval changed me, not only as a person but also as a professional therapist.

I never liked the idea of long-term therapy; I could not understand why it took people so long to heal. What I discovered in shamanism is that therapy takes so long because the part of the person that needs to be healed is not present and available for treatment. The lost soul part is in a different reality and is not even present in the therapy session.

When I first started my shamanic training, I asked my clients if they would allow me to do soul retrievals on them as experiments. All consented except for one individual who considered the concept too bizarre. Within one month, all of the consenting clients were finished with their therapy. The results were amazing. I now understood, at a different level, the concepts, theories, and explanations that I had applied in prior therapy sessions.

During traditional therapy, people often understand what has happened to them on an intellectual or cognitive level, but still change does not occur. They remain too attached to their pain. The shamanic explanation for this is that the lost soul part remains suspended in a different reality, reliving the traumatic event of its loss over and over. The client still does not have access to the soul part, and successful therapy is hindered by its absence. After a soul retrieval, there is understanding not only in the mind but also in the heart and soul of the client. The return of the lost soul part allows healing to occur emotionally, mentally, physically, and spiritually.

The soul is divine in its essence, and this divine nature is retained in a lost soul part. In receiving a soul retrieval, one never gets back the problem. The soul part left because of the problem. During the soul retrieval, the divine essence returns, which restores wholeness to the soul and causes the person to feel complete and empowered. The person is once again connected to his/her divine nature and able to detach from the past. Energy is no longer held captive to the past, and it is no longer necessary to relive the event and experience its pain.

After a soul retrieval, previous therapies increase in value and understanding. The multilevel healing allows the person to process information from the perspective of wholeness, rather than of fragmentation, and to move beyond the traumatic experience. As a result, perspectives about self and life change: When perspectives change, reality changes. It is then that life changes can occur.

Shamanic journeying is available to anyone willing to learn. (Refer to the chapter titled, "The Shamanic Journey," to learn how to do this.) The journey is a state of altered consciousness that is often induced by a sonic instrument such as the drum. Prior to the journey, the clients are asked about the intention of the journey, which is what they hope to gain from the experience. During the journey, the shaman meets up with his or her power animals—or spiritual allies—to gain information pertaining to the intention declared. Journeys take place in three different realms: The lower, upper, and middle worlds. The three worlds hold different kinds of information, and the shaman learns how to travel in these different realities. The knowledge gained is usually in the form of a metaphor, the meaning of which must be deciphered by the shaman and the client.[6]

In the beginning of my new work, I interlaced my shamanic journeys with my understandings of psychology. I explained to my clients how the journeys worked and how I was able to gather information about their soul loss. I still provide the psychological explanation for my clients, but these unordinary travels provide the greater understanding.

The journeys are real. The worlds where these journeys take me do exist. There is a profound magic to them that is literally unexplainable using traditional human thought systems and language. The more I realize the reality of these places and the energy contained in them, the more powerful my healing practice becomes and the more instantly things manifest in my own life.

The journey is used not only for the purpose of soul retrieval. It provides access to information from the spiritual realm as unlimited as the universe and the imagination. Anything is possible, and information is readily available. Although there are other ways to gather information from the spirits, the journey is the method I prefer and the one I teach my clients. My goal is to empower my clients to connect with their own spirit helpers. Who knows better than one's own spiritual teachers and one's own soul what is needed to heal and to grow? The spiritual realm is full of helping spirits and divine love; you just need to know how to access the information. Journeying is one door to that information.

In learning how to journey, I became increasingly aware of the spiritual realm—of other realities and dimensions. I realized that I had been blinded to these realities in the past because of the limited use of my senses. I discovered just how disconnected most human beings are to the energy and spirituality around them.

Reality is an illusive thing. People are most dependent on their eyes to gain information, but our human vision is remarkably limited. Even 20/20 vision in humans is paltry compared to that of many in the animal kingdom. Because of our obsession with sight, we have limited the use of our other senses and have diminished their potential effectiveness. The phrase, "I'll believe it when I see it," expresses well the limitation we place on ourselves. With that statement we consciously establish a barrier to fuller development.

We, as a culture, have overdeveloped the left side of our brains at the expense of the right side. Our schools, bureaucratic institutions, sciences, and our very culture have emphasized analytical understanding while minimizing the value of creativity. We have become what the spirits fondly refer to as lopsided. I often say to clients that some spiritual things simply cannot be explained in words. To explain in rational terms is to dilute the experience. Trying to explain a right brain, nonlinear experience using left-brain linear, analytical, sequential, and rational terms does not work. Spirit is the world of the nonlinear; it uses the senses of the soul, which are governed by the heart. It is often said that the shaman "sees," "hears," "feels," and "knows" with her/his heart. Journeying develops these "senses of the soul" while it stimulates and utilizes the right side of the brain.

As in anything, the more you practice journeying the better you will get at discovering new realities. New worlds open up that are blindly missed by the human eye and the rational left brain. I am amazed at what is available to all individuals when they let go of existing paradigms and limited perspectives. Opening the mind and allowing Spirit to work unencumbered is what we often call a miracle or magic. It is what Spirit calls "eagle vision" or "soul vision," the ability to rise above the limited view of immediate circumstance to gain a broader, more inclusive perspective. There is so much more to "see" in the universal picture when one uses the senses of the soul and lives by the heart.

[1] Michael Harner, *The Way of the Shaman* (San Francisco: Harper & Row, 1990).

[2-6] In these paragraphs I synthesize several ideas from the work of Sandra Ingerman both from workshops and her book, *Soul Retrieval: Mending the Fragmented*

Self (San Francisco: Harper & Row, 1991). I wish to express sincere thanks to both Sandra Ingerman and Michael Harner for their expertise and teaching. Although I have blended their ideas into much of my own thinking, I want to acknowledge their significant influence.

Life Experiences—Choice—Karma— Unconditional Love

The terms "life experiences," "choice," "karma," "and unconditional love" are all part of the same whole. I will explain them individually, in the way that I received them in my own teachings; however, they must be understood holistically. One without the other can bring confusion. Together, these terms explain the wonder of life.

Life Experience

Life is physical. We are born into a physical body, and we live in a physical world. We interpret our experiences physically. This physicality allows us to "feel," which the spirits have explained to me is the major component of the earth experience. The earth experience is one of emotion, where the soul acquires a physical understanding of emotion. For example, it is one thing to conceptualize anger and another thing to experience anger and to feel it throughout the body. The same holds true for love. It is significantly different to think about being in love and about the concept of love than it is to "feel" love and the emotions and physical sensations of love. When one thinks of the vast array of human emotions, one realizes how many lifetimes must be lived in order to "know" life.

It is the spirits' message that we live many lifetimes and experience many life forms and situations along our path to understanding. With each incarnation, your spirit selects the physical realities you will experience in that lifetime. You, embodied in your spirit, choose the circumstances you will be born into: the life conditions, the geographic location, the economic status, the handicaps, and the body type. You actually choose all of the fixed factors that will constitute a major portion of your *life experience.* You also choose your variable life conditions—those conditions that can change through growth and development as you progress through life. These choices constitute the conditions under which you live each lifetime. What you have chosen to experience is designed for a particular

32

unfolding of your soul. The choices are made at a spiritual level—a soulful, subconscious level—before you incarnate into this particular body. The unfortunate thing about being human is that you do not get to remember, consciously, the spiritual choices that you made before your incarnation. This lack of remembering, however, allows you to experience each life fully and completely in its current physical reality.

Choice

Choice, or free will, refers to how you choose to *relate* to your life's conditions. You can always choose your reaction to *any* given circumstance, which means that variables can change instantaneously with each choice. Your choices have direct impact on both your physical life and on the growth of your soul. Each lifetime will grant you a different perspective and facilitate new awareness. Each will provide physical experience for the soul. You may spend several lifetimes experiencing the hardships of life without any inclination to seek God or enlightenment; however, there will come a time when the soul asks you to wake up, to pay attention, and to look at the big picture of life. Questions like, "What is the purpose of life?" "Who am I?" and "What is God?" will arise in you. You will begin to search for answers. This may take many lifetimes and numerous answers, each with a variation of experience and exposure. In the end, every soul will reach enlightenment because every soul is a reflection of God.

You may wonder why anybody would choose negative life experiences like sexual molestation, alcoholism, or being born into warring or starving countries; however, each life has a divine plan with necessary experiences for the soul. All life experience adds to personal growth. No life is a waste; there are no mistakes. No lifetime is judged to be better than another because each is a chosen experience toward enlightenment.

A soul might choose to experience prejudice. You may have chosen to be a slave during the 1700's in the United States as one dimension of the experience of prejudice. Since the soul is seeking to know all dimensions, you may then have chosen a lifetime as a slave owner, and then as a Ku Klux Klan member, then a parent who lost a child to the Klan, then a person of interracial marriage, and then a parent of someone who chose to marry interracially. Every conceivable perspective of prejudice could be experienced. The lessons in each of these lifetimes become a part of the unfolding process of the soul.

You may currently be experiencing a lifetime with alcoholism—as the parent of an alcoholic, or the child, or the spouse, or the counselor, or as the alcoholic who dies from liver failure, or the alcoholic who survives and becomes reformed.

Whatever perspective you are living is part of the divine plan for you to experience and learn from.

Nothing is experienced singly; everything is interwoven with others who constitute your lifetime experience. Once you, as a soul, make the choice to experience a particular concept, other souls help you play out these experiences. They are often referred to as your "spirit family." We tend to experience life on earth with a particular group of souls, changing parts, or scripts, with each lifetime. You will find numerous links and interconnections with your family or circle of friends when you start to explore other lifetimes. It can be fun and healing. Behaviors, attitudes, and trauma can be understood more completely from the deeper historical perspective. Here is an example:

I was told a great true story the other day about a woman who was researching her genealogy. She traced her family line back to the era of the Civil War when her family served as slaves. She reached an impasse in her project, and was directed to a genealogy specialist. She and the specialist became great friends as they explored different aspects of her family's history. They developed a special bond and were both glad their lives had come together. As their investigation continued, they discovered that they shared a common history. The genealogist's ancestral family members were plantation owners during the Civil War, and, in fact, were the plantation owners where this woman's ancestral family served as slaves!

Coincidence you say? Hardly.

Many times, in the process of a soul retrieval, I will journey to a client's past life experience. A healing can be done in this past life reality that will actually affect my client's current life—a phenomenon that underscores that time is relative. The spirits have repeatedly told me that time is not linear but holographic, meaning that all things happen at the same moment but in different realities. This makes shamanic journeying for soul retrievals, or visiting different lifetimes, possible. The person doing the journey travels into that particular time dimension. The ability to cross into other dimensions means we can relive or view a past event and find healing in what we thought no longer existed. We can remember a future before it is present.

This multidimensional phenomenon is evident in the following story of Jim, who was struggling with a career decision. Jim's current career had started with the death of John Lennon. Jim was about 18 years old at the time of Lennon's death, but he had had a powerful experience at this time, which changed the course of his life. When Lennon died, Jim felt him enter his body. He committed himself to John's spirit, and became obsessed with learning all of his music. Jim is a talented musician and developed a very successful band, which played Beatle standards. This supported Jim, both financially and soulfully. But after many years, Jim felt as if he were becoming lost as an individual. He wanted to develop his own style of music and be recognized for himself. There came a time when Jim was ready to hang up his Sergeant Pepper's suit, but he had much indecision and remorse about this career change. He felt as though he were breaking his commitment to keep John and his music alive. He asked me to journey to John's spirit.

My spirit helpers almost always show me things metaphorically during a journey, somewhat like a dream. Luckily for me, my spirit helpers also usually explain the metaphors to me, unlike a dream where I must figure out the symbology for myself. The first scene that came to me in the journey was Jim lying on the floor sobbing into his hands. John walked up and pulled Jim to his knees. He then embraced him tightly. Jim continued to sob on John's shoulder with John supporting and consoling him.

The scene then changed to Jim and John flying through the air. Their bodies were actually blended, as if they were superimposed on each other. Each of them had one arm and leg free and off to the side, but their inside arms and legs were superimposed. John was about a head's length in front of Jim.

After several moments of this, the scene changed to Jim and John curling up into a ball, or sphere that appeared like rolling light. I then saw Earth off in the distance, as if I were viewing the planet from a space capsule.

I asked for an explanation of the metaphors. The first scene, where John was consoling Jim, had a real twist in it for my client. Jim had been a drug addict, and his involvement with John's music actually was part of his own healing. The Beatle band had kept Jim productive, responsible, and clean. In order to be a success, he had to take care of himself. John was actually keeping Jim alive, not the other way around.

The second scene, with them flying through the air superimposed, was explained as Jim and John actually being the *same soul expressed in two different incarnations at the same time!* Absolutely amazing! The reason that John's head was shown a head's length in front of Jim was that he was about 20 years older than Jim and further along in the expression of his life. I marveled at the meaning contained in such a simple image. I found it incredible. The spirits then went on to explain the imagery of the spherical ball of light that Jim and John had become. They stressed again, through this imagery, that time is not linear, it is holographic. There really is no such thing as past or future lives. Everything is happening simultaneously in different dimensions of time. Earth was used to illustrate that we can look at all individuals and see different incarnations of our soul being lived out. We have got a whole planet of people who are different expressions of us.

John Lennon's words from "I Am the Walrus" are interestingly appropriate to Jim's experience, like a message to him across time:

> I am he,
> and he is me,
> and we are all together.

Is this what the great masters and teachers such as Jesus, Buddha, and Muhammad have been implying for centuries? If so, I was beginning to understand it.

Since this journey, the spirits have expanded their teaching about incarnations. They fondly expressed to me that when we have real attachments to things, such as to a particular writer, poet, artist, or sculptor, and are drawn to his or her work, it is probably because we were actually the creator of that piece of work. If we read something from history that profoundly teaches us, we may have been part of the actual event. Even if we are extremely attached or moved to help someone, perhaps to support a child in a Third World country, then we are probably that child in a different lifetime expression. Do unto others as you would do unto yourself; the other might actually be you! Now there's a thought.

I am still processing this information and probably will be for several years to come. It is amazing. The spirits have since taught me to journey to my other lifetimes and to remember the wisdom I gained from each lifetime expression. I have also learned to journey to souls I would like to learn more about. The possibilities available through journeying are unlimited. Journeys to other lifetimes can be extremely informative, but also lots of fun. I highly recommend them for anyone practicing their journey skills.

We need to understand that lifetimes are both experiences of the soul and an exchange of energy. We also need to remember that *everything* is energy. Lifetimes are energy, and thoughts, words, and actions are energy. Everything is energy and everything affects and is affected by everything else. Energy used in a directive way is power.

The universe is in a constant state of motion striving to keep energy in balance. Even if we are not consciously aware of our energy and how it affects the whole universe, the universe is aware of it. We are all very powerful beings.

The actions of every person on the planet affect the lives of us all; one never does anything that is isolated from others. We are all interconnected in a divine sphere—relating, interrelating, and exchanging energy in a holographic and pro-found way. These interrelationships are extremely complex, coloring every experience we have.

I understand that this is a difficult concept because it is so vast, so I will describe it metaphorically:

> A butterfly hatches out of its cocoon 2,000 years ago.
> It sits in the sun in a far away country to dry its wings.
> It then begins to flap its wings, moving the air around its body.
> That movement of air alters the surrounding nature
> and the influences expand ever outward.
> That continuing effect of change creates our weather patterns today!

This metaphor is, in truth, an expression of the scientific principle of complexity. Quantum theory recognizes the complex association of interdependence as fundamental to reality. All of existence self-orders into a purposeful, yet unpredictable pattern. Science, however, "discovered" this reality long after it was known to mystics. In the study of spirituality, the manipulation of energy is fundamental. Directing energy in a powerful way through intention can be used for both good and evil. People can be harmed or healed through words that carry powerful intentions.

A woman called me to make an appointment for her daughter, who was having night terrors. Night terrors are different from nightmares in that the people experiencing them cannot be awakened. In fact, the more you try to awaken them, the deeper they travel into their terror. Often the sleeping person makes bone chilling, eerie sounds. The sleeping person may have eyes open or closed. If open, you can see soul-deep the horror of their experience. The night terror episode is terrorizing for all concerned.

There are many levels of experience in night terrors, but one thing holds true: the people experiencing them are traumatized, as are the ones who are trying to awaken them. Doctors have no cure, and drugs are ineffective. When my client brought me her child, she had tried everything else and decided to seek shamanic healing as a last resort.

The journey I am about to describe is one of the most revelatory I have experienced. It not only created a healing for this individual, but it also opened my eyes to the complexity of life, past lives, the power of words, and multifaceted healing.

During the journey I had an almost comical vision of an African scene. There was a little African warrior standing about two feet tall. He had on a grass skirt with grass pompoms around his ankles and wrists. He had on a black mask with grass hair, and he was carrying a spear. He approached me, screaming in what I assumed was an African language, waving his hands and spear around and stomping his feet. Even though I had no idea what he was saying, his body language was definitely angry and threatening. I felt like I needed the protection of my spirit allies.

I asked my power animals, "What is this all about?" I was told that the night terrors my client was experiencing were because of a black magic or voodoo spell that was placed on her soul in a different lifetime. The results of that spell were being played out through the night terrors. I was amazed but also perplexed and wondered what to do. I followed my spirit allies' instructions and, to my amazement, the little African image dropped his spear and was defused and powerless. The spell was broken.

Please remember, the images in a journey are metaphors; they are used to explain a situation and are usually not literal. The actual truth in this journey was that a spell or curse had been cast; we were dealing with negative forces put into action from human intention. (Humans do all kinds of awful things to each other.)

After breaking the spell, I continued with the journey to bring back any lost soul parts. There had been much soul loss and loss of power within my client because of the night terrors. The spirits made sure that all was in order before we left the journey.

After completing the soul retrieval, I spent time explaining to both my client and her mother what had happened during the journey. We then discussed the recommendations given to me by the spirits about how to facilitate her healing by calling in certain healing allies at night before bed. With this advice, the mother and daughter left my office.

After people leave my office, my normal procedure is to clean, with sage, the sacred items I used during the soul retrieval. As I was doing this, I heard a loud crash in the adjoining room. The floor shook and a strange energy surged up my spine. With my stomach fluttering, I ran out of my office to see what had happened. There on the floor lay an African mask that had fallen off of the wall. I stared at the mask in both disbelief and amusement. The fear that I momentarily felt surge through my body melted. My amusement came from an understanding I had developed through my longtime work with the spirits. I realized immediately that this mask had not accidentally fallen off the wall, but had more likely jumped off the wall to get my attention. I actually laughed out loud as I bent to pick up the mask, realizing how blatant the spirits can be to get one's attention. I also was keenly aware that there was a real similarity between the mask that hung on my wall and the one I encountered in the journey.

I found myself saying to the mask, "So what do you know about this black magic stuff I just encountered?"

I took the mask into my office and did a journey with it. During my journey with the mask, it gave me all kinds of information about spells, curses, the power of the spoken word, how to move energy to counter spells, and how to become invisible when I get myself into dangerous situations during a journey. In fact, I am to wear this particular mask in non-ordinary reality when I need to become invisible. The mask was letting me know that it was to serve a very important role in my life. I have since moved the mask into my office space where it serves many purposes. The mask has become a beloved ally in the spiritual realm. Its name is Legba.

Needless to say, I was astonished at this information, and I had a sudden epiphany. I realized that I had been prepared for years for this moment, for this client, for this teaching. I was prepared not only from my studies in shamanic healing but even in my decorating motif. I have collected tribal or indigenous art all of my adult life and all of my tribal art has been "danced." Danced is a term that means that the piece is not only original, but has actually been used in traditional ceremonies. This particular mask was the first in my collection. I have had this mask since I was 22 years old, and I can guarantee that when it came into my life I was unaware of shamanic healing or of what the mask was capable of doing. I wondered why I was interested in cultural artifacts. Why was I drawn to cultures around the world? Where did this interest originate? The mask came to me in a serendipitous way through various long-forgotten friends who had lived in Africa. I had admired the mask for years and they eventually gave it to me. It had hung on my wall for 20 years and had never fallen off!

I realize now that the mask came into my life for a reason—in preparation for this very moment. It is a reminder of the divine order of the universe. Nothing is out of place and every interaction, every friendship, every encounter, every thing is divinely ordered and interrelated. All this time I had thought I was selecting my own artwork, but in truth it was selecting me.

Since this experience, other things (art pieces, fetishes, altar icons) have spoken to me and allowed me to understand their divine purpose in my life and the part they play in my chosen path. I no longer doubt my own purpose, or question how someone raised in traditional American ways could have such a profound connection to the spiritual realm and magic of indigenous cultures. I accept that it is so.

Why do we choose the things we do? Why do we buy the things we buy? Why do we marry the people we marry? All are part of our life plan, part of what we are destined to experience. Why worry that we are making the right choices when there are no wrong choices. There is an incredible divine plan that we helped create. Our lives are not a jumbled bag of accidents, failures, and missed opportunities. All things are just as they should be. Not even a grain of sand in all the universe is out of order or not loved unconditionally.

My client with night terrors suffered from a spell created by another's curse. This is an example of an extreme in negative energy, but the lesson for all of us is that words carry energy. The negativity we might project onto another acts like a curse, carrying the power to hurt and damage. This could even continue, as in the case of my client, through multiple lifetimes. Words are energy, and they carry with them the energy of their intention until the energy is transformed by a countervailing intention. Negative energy has an impact on the speaker *and* the person it is directed toward, with energetic (karmic) repercussions that can be devastating. Use care in your words and consider fully your intention.

Karma

There is always a reaction to any action; nothing goes unnoticed. Many would call this balancing of energy "karma." Colloquially, it might be expressed as, "what goes around, comes around." The golden rule: "Do unto others as you would have them do unto you," is another expression of this action-reaction concept. Another way to describe this law of the universe is, as Elizabeth Haich writes in her book, *Initiations*: "When we strike our hand against a wall, the wall strikes back without intending to! It is not the wall, which really strikes back, but our own blow bounces back. In any case, whatever we hit always gives back the same blow we gave it."

Karma is not about punishment; it is about energy. Remember, every thought, word, and action consists of energy. You activate this energy. Think of Newton's third law of energy: For every action there is an equal reaction.

If you think, speak, and act negatively, this same energy will come back to you. The same holds true if you think, speak, or act positively out of love. The more you create a positive, loving state of energy, the more you will experience this in return. Karma is a field of energy. It surrounds individuals and seeks balance. People who see energy or auras know that energy, generated from within the body, is evident around the person and extends into the aural field.

During the process of one of my soul retrieval journeys, I came across something that appeared as a dark, looming cloud of energy surrounding my client. I asked my spirit helpers about this energy, and they informed me that it was karma, which had accumulated around this particular person. I shuddered because it looked awful and had the feel of anger and hatred. I immediately thought that we needed to leave this negative energy alone. I believed that others' karma should not be interfered with because it was part of their destiny. (I had always heard that karma, as described in books and by other people, was something a person was stuck with and had to live out.)

My spirit helpers said to me, "Jan, are you here to follow your human rules, or are you here to do a healing?"

I was dumbfounded. Never did I expect a comment like that from my spirit helpers. I realize now that this journey was an important turning point in my learning. The spirits used this journey to help me understand that "punishment" is a human concept. The spirits never inflict punishment; they love all beings unconditionally. My spirit helpers taught me repeatedly that all karma is healed through love, as love instantaneously heals and balances all energies. Loving yourself and loving others will create change in the most adverse situations. Remember, there is no experience that is less or more important than another; there is no lifetime better or worse than another. Each life circumstance comes with its own set of challenges and experiences, and all are part of the exquisite whole.

Karma is not hung on you like a scarlet letter; however, you do build an energy around you. This energy accumulates and is always in motion, as it tries to maintain balance with other energies. Sometimes this balancing is quick; sometimes it will take years; sometimes it flows into other lifetimes, but it will balance. If ever you question why certain things are happening to you, take some time to look at what you are doing and thinking.

You can change your life, by changing your thoughts, your words, and your actions. At any time, you may choose the path of enlightenment. All negative life situations, all fear, can be balanced and reversed through love. You can choose to open the heart, forgive, let go, and be happy. No matter what your past, love heals. Even in situations where you find no reasonable explanation for why things happen the way they do, your life can change.

We are not stuck with disastrous lives or having to live out a particular karma if we choose to change our thinking away from fear and judgments. So much of our thinking keeps unfortunate things in motion. If you are experiencing, or have experienced, many struggles and hardships in your lifetime, you can be assured you are *not* being punished or held in an unmerciful way by some judgmental God. You can also be assured that there is a bigger picture being played out with your life than that represented by current circumstances. There is a divine plan designed uniquely for you that is based in unconditional love. Judgments prevent you from seeing life from a holistic view, and they keep you caught in your pain. The same holds true for unforgiveness. The failure to forgive imposes chains on the heart of the unforgiving. Forgiving is always for self. It clears the energy field instantaneously. Try it. You will see what I mean. When one forgives another, there is a physical, emotional, and spiritual freedom for both the giver and receiver. Forgiveness, like love, heals two souls at once.

So let me recap. The soul is vast, it is immortal, and it adheres to no timeline. Each lifetime could be represented like an individual word on a page of an enormously long novel. Life creates the story, filled with romance and loneliness, gain and loss, terror and glee, destruction and creativity, betrayal and glory, wealth and poverty, royalty and destitution. All facets of life are experienced wholly, and each lifetime is valuable. Everything necessary to create wholeness for your soul is present. Each lifetime follows the laws of the universe—creating, co-creating, accumulating, being.

The ultimate goal of the soul is to seek, to experience, and to understand the marvelous wonder of existence. Enlightenment is achieved when one finds perfection and unconditional love in all experiences. This progresses through eons of time, with each lifetime gaining, unfolding, and developing new awareness—every experience of every lifetime adds to the whole of the soul. You are forever expanding and accumulating information consciously and unconsciously. Although our physical being does not, the soul remembers in perfect detail every experience ever had; every thought ever thought; every word, feeling, smell, scene, and taste ever known. It all is categorized and remembered. This creates a particular energy: The energy of *you*.

There is a cause and effect inherent in everything, including thoughts. The soul not only seeks experience, it also seeks itself. The soul is the divinity of God and unconditional love incarnate. The secret of life is not in pointing fingers at everybody else and judging their behaviors or beliefs, but in looking closely at self and noticing what choices you make for yourself and where those choices take you. Are they based in fear or love? Are they for your highest good? Are you adding positively or negatively to life as a whole, including all life on the planet? This, my friend, is a full time job. Do not worry about what you have done; stay focused on what you are doing. Karma is balanced through love. Love is the most powerful and greatest energy of the universe, and it will positively affect even the most adverse situations. It is the ultimate healer. It is God. It can be used to heal and balance any situation in the universe.

The universe is based on and created from love. Anything not of love will create an imbalance, and the universe will strive to put this energy into balance. This balancing is not about punishment and reward, but it is about natural consequences. Striking out at others, grievances, unforgiveness, hatred, violence, anger, fear, and jealousy all have an energy to them, and there will be a reaction if this is the energy you choose to display. This energy is real and will affect you even if your attitudes remain as thoughts only. You will feel the effects of your negative attitudes and actions because they will become enormous obstacles to the growth of your soul. Make note that I am not saying these attitudes are wrong, but that they do constitute an extremely dense energy that will inhibit your own enlightenment. Remember, to seek enlightenment is to seek love.

The enlightenment of the soul is based in love and walking the spiritual path from the heart. Being aware and conscious means making deliberate choices to exhibit love, no matter what situation or life condition you find yourself in. This change always involves personal work and commitment to the process of change. It can be complex, and you may feel like you are beating your head against a wall. Truly, the soul is complex, vast, immortal, interconnected, and multifaceted. This makes healing and change also complex and vast. However, when you are working with love as a tool, you are using the most powerful force in the universe, and the results can be miraculous.

I have personally found that when I feel blocked in my own growth, it is often wise to seek someone who works with energy and is not invested in my personal issues. This helps achieve clarity. Spiritual growth can often be facilitated by someone who works with energy and the healing of the soul. In some situations, our obstacles might stem from soul loss that occurred earlier in life or from circumstances of another lifetime and are not present in our conscious mind. The spirits have taught me that the care of the soul is the first concern, and that the soul is a composite of all that you have ever experienced in all lifetimes. This complexity of the soul creates multilevels of healing and makes growth possible.

The Universal Laws of Energy and Change

Change occurs when energy shifts. In order to understand change, one needs to understand the dynamics of energy. Everything emanates energy—animate beings, physical objects, even thoughts and feelings—and these energy "fields" impact and alter all they touch. If we are to have control over the changes in our lives, we must also understand the importance of thoughts, beliefs, ideas, and feelings, as energy. Only when we understand and can apply these basic laws of the universe will we be able to consciously affect the change process:

1. Energy follows intention.

2. Whatever you add energy to, multiplies.

3. Thought followed by word and action equals form.

4. What you believe, becomes.

These laws apply to all of life and are fundamental in understanding how to work with energy in order to create. Healing, both of self and others, is possible by developing skills in working with these laws. Enlightenment requires this understanding.

People with spiritual power have learned how to work with energy by following the guidelines of these laws. They can direct energy with intention and trust that the desired outcome will materialize. They are not victims of other people or situations because they know how energy works and they apply this knowledge to their lives. The following explanations address each of these laws separately; however, they are practiced as a unit of truths. A holistic approach is an absolute necessity.

Energy follows intention.

What is intention? It is simply what you intend to happen. If your intention is followed with an action that supports your intention, you will experience quick results. You will also feel good and harmonious in the process. It is as if all energy flows in the same direction. For example, let's say that your intention is to work on your marriage by being more attentive to your partner. If your action is to start a productive conversation, give a foot rub, or make a phone call during the day, the desired outcome of improving your marriage has a high probability of occurring. If your intention is to improve your marriage, but you do extremely inconsiderate things to your partner, the energy of your action is in opposition to your intention. This opposite flow of energies will cause much friction, anxiety, and stress.

Look at the illustration below from an energy flow standpoint.

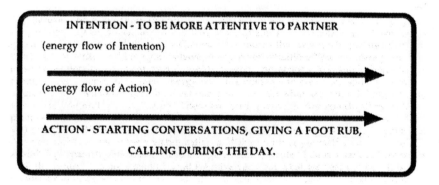

When both the intention and action flow in the same direction (as above) positive outcome is enhanced. But when intention and action flow in opposite directions (as below), negative outcome is more likely.

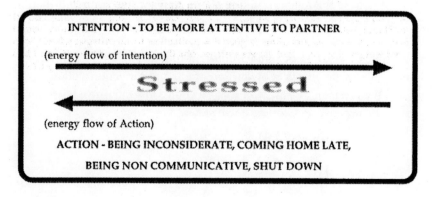

Conflicting energy signals will cause frustration, stress, and anxiety. Opposite directional forces between intention and action remind me of the opposite motions of the earth's plates at the San Andreas Fault line. As the plates move against each other, they create tremendous stress and, ultimately, result in an earthquake. Just as the spirits always tell me, "Learn from nature!"

You can use this energy illustration as a mental cue for anything you are attempting to change in your life. Write down your intention, and then look at the actions you follow it with. Are they flowing together or in opposite directions? Many people give lip service to wanting to create change or healing in their lives, but their actions do not match their intention. They often become frustrated with the process of change, feeling like they have failed again when, in truth, their actions are not aligned with their intentions. Either the action needs to change or the intention needs to change. Each one can correct either variable and obtain positive results.

Whatever you add energy to, multiplies.

This is a literal statement. It is both a physical law as well as a universal law, which basically explains how we create. Creator has given you free will, or sacred choice. This means that you freely choose what you think, say, or write, and how you behave in any given situation. You create your existence—literally—by your own thoughts, words, and actions. You think thousands of thoughts per second, all of them energy with the potential to create an actual physical manifestation. Whatever gets the most energy—wins. So what are you thinking all day? Where are you multiplying energy? These are hard questions. Are you dwelling in the past, giving wrong deeds or past hurts the energy to constantly recreate their pain? Are you angry or self-loathing, causing unfortunate situations to keep recurring in your life? Are you thinking about your victimization and then finding yourself a victim once again? The Spanish philosopher, Jose Ortega y Gasset, wrote "Life is a series of collisions with the future; it is not a sum of what we have been but what we yearn to be." It is important to understand our past but not to dwell on it. We create ourselves by our intentions and the actions following those intentions. We create our future. We make a choice to see positive possibilities or to dwell in the negative. A Chinese poem states:

> If the water of the Tsanglang is clear,
> I will wash the ribbon of my hat.
> If it is dirty, I will wash my feet in it.

If you choose to see positive results, you will begin the process of creating a positive future. You will literally create your life situations. The reverse is also true. If you dwell on the negative about a situation and are worrying about it, talking about it negatively, and being the victim of it, you will add negative energy to it. Energy is the fuel for creation, but there is a human choice as to where it will be applied.

Remember:

Whatever You Add Energy to, Multiplies

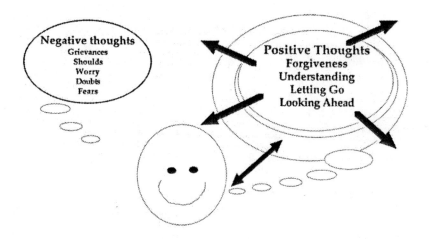

Where are you placing the most energy? Which side is multiplying?
Think of this energy as a cloud—
a physical mist of energy that is surrounding you.
Every thought counts; you are feeding one side or the other.

Thought followed by word and action equals form.

This law is an extension of the previous law—whatever you add energy to, multiplies. However, this law is about the *amount* of energy present in a given situation. There is a significant variation in energy from one circumstance to another. Thoughts function initially at a low frequency. When we attach spoken or written words to thoughts, we increase their energy frequency. Speaking and writing add additional form to thoughts. What may have been a random thought assumes more explicit form. In other words, intention is more clearly defined and given form. You may have noticed that when you explain something to others, it becomes much clearer to yourself. This is because your random thoughts become organized and take the form of statement. This takes energy, which is then stored in the words. Words, as speech and script, are powerful. They become like contracts with the universe, and should be taken seriously.

Taking action or putting energy into motion is the follow through for what is thought or said. Intention manifests into action and creates. In other words, thought followed by words and action equal form. This equation can be applied to something as minor as baking a cake or to a major endeavor such as building a house. Everything ever invented began with a thought, which was then put into words, and then translated into action, which resulted in the invention materializing, or taking form. After the thought, words, and action followed, something materialized. The process of enlightenment, or becoming spiritually connected, follows the same pattern. You have the thought that becoming more aware is what you would like for yourself. You speak of this to others, and you take action by reading books, listening to teachers, journeying to spirit, and so forth. The end result is a changed you—a new form.

What you believe, becomes.

The writer Anais Nin wrote: "We do not see things as they are, we see things as we are." Not only are you a reflection of your thoughts, but also the world you see around you is created by your thoughts. There is an ancient Chinese proverb: "When you have a cart and a horse you have three things—a cart, a horse, and a cart and horse."

The interdependence and integration of all things results in the whole being greater than the sum of the parts. To understand the parts is not to fully understand the whole, for the whole is much more. Belief systems consist of individual thoughts and attitudes, but they also are more than the sum of these. Conflict and contradiction in our thoughts creates a dysfunctional whole. Clarity comes as the mind, spirit, and body achieve an alignment.

Underlying every thought, every word, and every deed is your belief system. What do you really believe about life, about yourself, about God? Belief systems are complex. They are your core—fundamental to your entire being. Belief systems will directly influence every facet of your life. Do you really know what you believe or how you came to believe it? Most people are not aware of how they obtained their belief systems. Many are handed down from parents, schools, churches, cultures, societies, and other environments. Christianity influences persons born in the United States because it is the predominant religion of the country, just as a person born in India would have a Buddhist or Hindu influence. If you travel around the world, you will come in contact with different belief systems that create completely different realities. Cultures are built, and wars are fought because of belief systems.

Part of becoming awake and aware is to discover what you believe. Belief systems make you think, say, feel, and behave in certain ways. If you work backward from your behaviors, you will always find a core belief that controls your behavior. But belief systems are choices, and they can be changed. You need to determine if your beliefs are supporting or blocking your healing and growth. One person can change a belief and, in turn, change the world. As Ghandi said, "We must be the change we want to see in the world." In order to do this, you need to explore your belief systems in great detail, get to the root of their existence, and then decide what changes you want to make.

If you understand the laws of energy, you can understand the process of creation, and then be directive in what you create in your life. If you are directive, you are utilizing your gift of choice—your sacred free will—to choose the personal thoughts and beliefs that will manifest in your life. When you realize the power of your thoughts, and start to monitor them, you have taken the first step toward creating change for yourself.

Constant monitoring of self is required for heightened awareness. People struggle when they seek to be this accountable because it requires deliberate and constant attention. However, this struggle is important, and it is the first step toward enlightenment. Although there are tools you can use to heighten awareness, such as books, affirmations, mantras, chanting, support groups, and churches, you must consciously monitor what you are thinking or you can negate much of your effort and your healing. People who are awake pay attention to their thoughts. Their attention is centered. They consciously evaluate where they direct their energy and whether their thoughts are serving their highest good. This is a huge undertaking, but the results can be phenomenal.

Let me give you an elementary example. Bring your attention to your breathing right now. Where is it centered in your body? Is it in your lungs or down in your belly? It is heavy or light? Are you breathing out of your mouth or nose? As you scan your body with your thoughts, you move energy and become aware of an automatic process. You can, by thought and intention, redirect your breathing and your body's response. Your body's energy changes as your thoughts change.

You are, at this very moment, evaluating my example and forming an opinion about it. Your opinion is also energy. Choosing to gain from an exercise will result in a positive outcome or feeling; choosing to think negatively about an exercise will have an adverse effect. You respond to your opinion on an energetic level. Remember *everything* is energy, including an opinion, which takes form in your thoughts. It springs out of your underlying belief system. Part of this quest is to discover where your opinions come from. In order to do that, you need to look at your basic belief system.

I have found that most people have a belief system that is based on their worth or lack of. Worthiness, being accepted, and being loved are major core belief structures that can fuel our *every thought and action,* including something as basic as an opinion about an exercise in a book.

As you walk the spiritual path and become more conscious, you will scrutinize your feelings, behaviors, and belief system. You will continually ask yourself, "Where is that thought coming from? What made me act that particular way? Why do I feel the way I do about that certain topic or individual?" You will learn to detach from your emotions and view yourself as an observer.

The laws help you understand how energy and creation work. You cannot *not* be creating. Every thought that you have is part of the creation process. Changing your life to become what you ultimately desire starts with self. Heal yourself first. Spirit has taught me that the only way you can truly heal yourself or reach your fullest potential is to *take a long good look at yourself and keep looking.* Detach and observe yourself.

Human thought and behavior is activated either by love or fear. Which of these two emotions governs you? If you are not living a life of joy, of peace, of self-confidence, you can be assured that your underlying belief system is based in fear.

All behavior, all invention, all change, and all creation starts with an intention followed by energy. Intention is moving energy with purpose. Intention connected to a deliberate action can have incredible force. To insure this force operates for the good of oneself and others, you must be sure that you are acting out of love and not from fear.

Being conscious is applying this law with intention. Creation is always happening. It either happens *to* you, or you can make it happen *for* you. If you are consistently wondering why a certain thing is happening to you, think again. You have free choice. Moment by moment you apply energy to your thoughts. Where is that energy going, and what are you creating for yourself? Your attitude and life reflect your choices. You are in control. This is the difference between being unconscious of the process of creation or being conscious and directive. You cannot *not* be creating.

If you are constantly saying,
"I never have enough time,"
guess what will be the result.

∞

If you are a worrier, are you putting your energy
into the outcome you desire or into your fear?
Worrying clearly works to your disadvantage and
can actually manifest your fears.

∞

If your constant thought is,
"I never have enough money,"
you never will.

Attitude

The longer I live, the more I realize the impact
of attitude on life.
Attitude, to me, is more important than facts,
it is more important than the past,
than education,
than money,
than circumstances,
than failures,
than success,
than what other people think
or say or do.

It is more important than appearance,
giftedness or skill.
It will make or break a company...
a church...a home...

The remarkable thing is we have a choice
every day regarding the attitude we will
embrace for that day.

We cannot change our past...
We cannot change the fact that people will
act in a certain way.
We cannot change the inevitable.
The only thing we can do is to play on the one
string we have,
and that is our attitude...
I am convinced that life is 10 percent
what happens to me
and 90 percent how I react to it.
And so it is with you...

—Charles Swindoll

Belief Systems, Attitude and Change

I, like many, spent several years in therapy. I had varying degrees of success, but I still viewed my childhood as something that wounded me terribly. I spent much of my adult life healing.

I was in a workshop, one day, and we were asked to come up with a happy memory from our childhood and to hold it in our minds as we continued with the exercise. I searched and searched for a happy memory. If an event presented itself with even an inkling of happiness, it proceeded to run itself out in my mind to a disastrously unhappy conclusion. I had no purely happy memory. I, of course, felt like I was the only person in the whole group who could not get a happy memory, which magnified my unworthiness issues. It was awful. I realized that instead of healing in my years of therapy, I had learned to understand what had happened at an intellectual and behavioral level, but I was still feeling much pain. I had a hole in my soul, and my spirit felt fragmented. As time went on, my spiritual life developed more, and I was introduced to extremely different philosophies from those I had been raised with. New awareness filled my being. I started to understand that I had choice in this earth-walk, and that the experiences I had as a child were ones I had chosen in order to develop my soul and myself.

I began to review my life from the perspective of choice. I had the choice to view my life's experiences with judgments of blame and remorse, or to view them as opportunities for growth. Eventually I saw the bigger picture of my life's experiences. This "eagle vision," as I was later taught to call it, is the ability to see personal experiences distantly but holistically.

What was my soul working on in this lifetime? What were the patterns? What was I continually recreating in my life at a subconscious level that allowed me the opportunity to choose a higher level of being? Was my soul evolving in a good way, or was I stuck in my own predetermined drama? Bitterness, victimization, anger, and grudges are all choices that trap the soul and prevent it from growing. They inhibit the soul like a jail inhibits freedom. Understanding this, I consciously chose to see my entire childhood differently and to view my life as experiences that promoted the choice for my soul to evolve into a higher state of being.

Years later, I found myself in a group setting again. This time, we were asked to write a story about an event in our childhood. I know that the intention of this assignment was to process again the events that had led us all to counseling. But this time I had a totally different perspective.

I wrote a story about a great fishing trip we had taken as a family and how much fun we had, how my family had such a spirit of adventure, and how many fabulous opportunities I had as a child. It was amazing what poured out of me. I had such a profound realization. I knew that my past had not changed, but my perspective on it had. The American psychologist William James once observed, "People can alter their lives by altering their attitudes." Those unhappy negative experiences, which I had dwelled on for so many years, took on the new flavor of being opportunities to learn how to love myself and others, how to claim my own worthiness, how to step away from the judgments of what others had done to me, and how to be thankful for the success in developing my own soul.

This was a huge step forward in my own development. It was not the writing assignment that caused this shift in focus, but it brought it to my awareness. In the time between the two workshops, I had chosen to change my belief system. I had adopted a philosophy that created healing. With this shift in my perception, I was able to internalize at an intellectual, emotional, behavioral, and spiritual level. My life has been extremely different ever since.

Another powerful example of attitude occurred when I was working with a client. I greeted my client as he arrived for his appointment, and realized immediately that he had a severe problem. His head was down, and his arms dangled at his sides. He was completely slumped over, and his eyes were closed. When I asked what was wrong, I received no answer. He came through the door, slowly, very slowly, dragging his feet and holding on to the railing with extreme effort and difficulty. It took him fifteen minutes to get in the door and to the chair in my office where he finally collapsed.

Eyes still closed, slumped in the chair to almost a fetal position, chin resting on his chest. He sat exhausted from the effort of entering my office. I was being shown, quite literally, how terrible he felt—the fatigue, the pain, the exhaustion of movement, the weariness of being alive. I watched him with concern. After a few moments of sitting in silence and listening to his arduous breathing, I asked a few questions but got a barely audible response, "I can't, it is too hard."

I finally asked my client to say the words, "I can" for one minute. I said with authority, "Begin."

He started mumbling the words, slowly repeating the phrase as directed. After about 25 seconds, he opened his eyes and his body started to move. His shoulders came up, he straightened his back, his head came up, and he actually looked at me. His voice was now stronger and clearer. At the end of the minute, his entire attitude, disposition, and posture had changed. It was amazing.

We then talked about what had created his burden of depression. It was fear—his fear of the future and of not being able to handle the changes and the challenges confronting him. His fear monopolized his thoughts, literally crippling him with fatigue. He had been saying, "I can't, I can't, I can't," and those words were destroying his life.

This simple experiment to change the negative thought and the words he was saying to himself, changed his entire energy. My client literally transformed in front of my eyes. His life situation was still physically the same, but his attitude toward it was different. We continued the session with a new hope.

Granted, this did not solve his problems, but it confronted the "I can't" attitude, which was destroying his life. He had been physically displaying the manifestation of his thoughts. I had a choice either to enable his woe, comforting his obvious distress, or remind him of his other choice. The task was not mine, but his. He had to experience firsthand the power of his thoughts and how he could be in control. His physical condition was in direct response to what he had been saying to himself.

Thoughts will either support you or destroy you. Try the following experiment with yourself:

Every morning when you wake up start saying,
"I can"
for one minute.

∞

When you are driving to work in the morning say,
"I can"
for one minute.

∞

Before you walk into a meeting, say
"I can"
for one minute.

∞

What are you telling yourself now? What beliefs are creating your reality?

Discover What Belief Systems Control Your Behavior

The following is an exercise, or process, you can use to explore the depths of your being. It is an exercise to discover your belief systems—what you believe to be true about yourself, about God, about life.

All of your actions are rooted in your belief system. Although most of your beliefs were formed as a child, they are in fact a choice. If you do not like what you believe, you can change it. As an adult, you have full control of your beliefs. In order to change, however, you must take a long, scrutinizing look at your particular belief structure.

Probe closely into your childhood beliefs. Look for the strong messages you received as a child. You may not yet realize that these strong messages usually constitute a major portion of your core belief structure and hold an incredible amount of power. Write these beliefs, or messages, down on paper in a list form. Keep the sentences short for easy reading. Again, you are searching for the core or foundation of a belief, not the philosophy behind it. After you have completed your list, write down what you would rather believe, what you would rather have heard as a child. This is the time to be co-creative and to use your imagination to construct a list that is *ideal.* Create the perfect God in your mind and on the paper—a belief system that will support you, love you, and work for you, not against you. There are no rules, except that you do this exercise in its entirety.

The following is a composite of the common belief statements I hear from my clients:

Common Beliefs about God from Childhood

1. God is external, lives in heaven, and is separate from myself.

2. God is male and has male characteristics.

3. God has lots of rules. I had better not break a rule or I will be punished.

4. God does not always give me what I want. I have to deserve it, and if I mess up. He will hold it against me.

5. I can only pray for the will of God. If my prayer does not line up with His will, my prayer will not be answered.

6. I am selfish if I pray for myself and God does not like it when I do. Besides, I am too unworthy to pray for myself.

7. God punishes me and withholds my prayers to teach me a lesson. I deserve hard lessons.

8. God gets disappointed in my behavior.

9. God has human feelings such as anger, disappointment, revenge, and judgment.

10. There is only one way to God and heaven, and that is through Christianity.

11. All things in the Bible are true in the literal sense.

12. I need to be respectful of God. If I do not pray "right," my prayers will not be answered.

13. God watches over me with a critical eye, seeing all the things I do. He waits for me to mess up, so that he can teach me another lesson.

14. It will be difficult to enter heaven if I do not keep God first and follow the rules.

15. I deserve to have it tough in life because I have done lots of bad things.

16. Mommy and Daddy say that God will not like me if I lie, cheat, steal, or do not brush my teeth.

17. If I do not believe just the way I am taught, I will burn in hell.

18. God is strict, but it is because I am undeserving and he is trying to teach me to be good.

19. Even though I am struggling financially, it is wrong to pray for money.

20. If I have money, I should give most of it away in order to show how grateful I am.

21. God disapproves of sex and shakes his head in disgust at me.

22. I do not think God likes me much. He does not show up very often.

Any person living with the above beliefs is going to have tremendous *fear* in his or her life. The whole system is based on judgment, fear, punishment, and *not being good enough*. It is structured on conditional love with strings attached to behavior. It would be difficult to find happiness under this system. The constant pressure from judgment alone would cause dis-ease to settle in the body. These beliefs stifle personal growth, imagination, and creativity. There is no foundation for self-worth to grow and develop.

As you review your list and discern the nature of your current belief system, remember that it represents choice. If it does not reflect what you desire, discard it. Let your imagination go and create a new belief system. Make a new list of what such a belief system could look like. Perhaps, it would look like this:

An Example of an Ideal Belief System

1.   My God lives within me. I am part of God and God is part of me.

2.   God has no gender, but is the essence of all things.

3.   There is no right or wrong, good or bad, no punishment. There is a karmic balancing, consistent and founded in divine unconditional love.

4.   I have complete choice in my behaviors without being judged.

5.   God is love—unconditional—and this love is the basis of the universe. God loves all.

6.   There is no right or wrong way to believe. All religions lead to the center, which is God.

7.   Heaven is not a place that you go to; it is an attitude of the divine. Live and experience heaven in the now.

8.   God is available to me in all circumstances. I am never without God. God is part of me.

9.   I have full responsibility, as a co-creator with God, for all that I AM and all that is around me.

10.   I am honored and revered in the universe.

11.   I am a spirit having an earth experience. It is one of many experiences in the universe. My soul's purpose on earth is to experience emotion.

12.   I choose my life experience, like an actor choosing a script in a play. I choose everything about my living conditions for the divine purpose of my soul's unfolding.

13.   All of my prayers are answered. My job as co-creator is to be clear with my intention so that my prayers can manifest.

14.   There is abundance for all in the universe. If I have abundance in my life, it does not mean that someone else must go without.

15.   I believe in miracles!

16. I am part of an exquisite whole. I am related to all life. I belong.

17. Angels can fly because they take things lightly.

A person with the above belief system is going to have a completely different outlook on life. Self-worth, self-empowerment, choice, unconditional love, honor, balance, and freedom will be reflected throughout the life of this individual. *What one believes, becomes.*

All experiences filter through your belief system. Ten people could have the same experience and all ten would have a different account of the experience and what it meant. Experience is filtered through individual belief systems that flavor everything in life.

Your lists may look entirely different from the two examples that I gave. That is good. In fact, you need to develop your own personal profile. These are just examples to trigger your own thinking. The important thing is to remember that whatever beliefs you choose will manifest into your own reality as you add energy to them. Be good to yourself. Give yourself the best and have fun with this assignment.

This is the first step in the process of bringing a new belief system into reality. In the beginning, it may feel uncomfortable, but let that be. Use your imagination and create. Give yourself permission to explore and create new possibilities. If you cannot imagine something as being possible, then you are not going to have it. But if you can imagine the possibility, you are already on your way to creating it. Your new belief system may even feel comfortable, like a familiar truth that automatically resonates with your soul. If this happens, realize that your soul is responding to a truth and letting you know about it through a feeling.

Remember to keep putting energy into your new belief. Buy books that will reinforce it, talk about it, gather with people of like minds—all of these acts will add energy to the new beliefs and help them to multiply. Do not be victimized by old belief systems handed to you as a child, especially if they are causing hardships in your life now. Do something about it.

Another area interfering with people's lives is their belief around money. These are excellent beliefs to scrutinize. What do you really believe about money, yourself, and God? Do your beliefs limit your access to money and a more comfortable life?

Limiting Beliefs about Money

1. There are limited amounts of money in the universe. If one person has it that means someone else does not.

2. The more I make, the more I should give away. If I keep a lot for myself, then I am being selfish.

3. There is something evil about money. (It is easier for a camel to pass through the eye of a needle than for a rich man to go to heaven.)

4. God only loves the meek and poor.

5. I have to work hard for my money.

6. I am really not deserving of money; I do a lot of wrong things.

7. My karma in this lifetime is to struggle; I always struggle with money.

8. I am not worthy of the easy life.

9. The only way I will get rich is if I win the lottery, and what are my chances of that? Only lucky people win the lottery.

10. I really believe in the unlimited resources of the universe, but when it comes to money, those concepts just do not seem to work.

11. I am stuck in a job I hate, but there is no other way to make money.

12. Trusting the universe to supply is fine, if I am doing well. But when it comes to making money, I need to take care of myself and not trust God. That's not being responsible.

13. It is wrong to pray for money.

The list of examples could go on and on. Do any of these beliefs ring true for you?

Alternative Beliefs That Open Access to Abundance:

1. There is abundance for all. Abundance for one does not mean lack for another.

2. The universal supply is infinite.

3. I can create what I want using energy and thought to produce results. My results can exceed anything I ever obtained through purely physical effort.

4. Money is a form of energy, which follows the same laws as all other forms of energy.

5. I am worthy to receive.

6. My worth is not related to how much money I make.

7. I love what I do for my life's work. The energy I put into creation of this work will bring me abundance and will make a contribution to the greater good of mankind.

8. This can be the most joyous, prosperous, and creative time in my life.

9. I am the source of my abundance. Through working with my feelings, beliefs, thoughts, and intentions, I can become a master at creating whatever I want.

10. Having things is not as important as mastering the process of creating them.

11. I deserve, I deserve, I deserve the best in life.

12. I trust that God is concerned about my money issues and I can pray about money.

Self-worth and the quality of deserving are at the core of every money issue I have ever encountered while working with a client. Look closely at what you really believe about yourself. Again, underlying belief systems can be hidden from immediate view, but we can discover (or uncover?) them. Be honest with yourself. You may need to start at the very core to understand how you truly feel about yourself—your self-love. No matter where you are on your spiritual path, keep looking at the issue of love. Love is what the universe is based on—you must not lose sight of this. Love includes self-love. In fact, self-love is the most important. When you love yourself, you will make quality decisions for yourself, which will directly influence every other relationship you have, including your relationship with money.

Energy Is Electrical and Magnetic

An energy field surrounds everything. Energy pulses out from objects, inter-acting with and absorbing other energies. A person's energy field, commonly called an aura, is generated inside the body and extends outward to surround it. Understanding the electrical and magnetic nature of energy is important to understanding healing.

The energy field you generate is created by your beliefs and thoughts. Like a radio tower, you send out concentric pulses of energy that broaden and weaken as they move farther away. An electromagnetic charge exists immediately around your body. This magnetism impacts all it comes in contact with and, by exten-sion, influences the entire universe. Like a strong magnet, your field of energy draws other energies to it and absorbs the power of them. The energies you attract and the ways they are absorbed are influenced by your belief systems. Your beliefs filter and alter other energies as they enter your power source and, in turn, become part of the energy that emanates from you.

This magnetic power draws to you the situations, people, and events that will reinforce whatever it is you believe. If you believe you are a victim, that people constantly exploit you and that you are unlovable, your electromagnetic field will be charged with those beliefs and will draw to you circumstances that reinforce this. If you believe you are a divine being, that all doors of opportunity are open to you, that you are loved by yourself and others, and that good things always come your way, then your magnetic energy will draw to you positive life condi-tions, which reinforce your positive energy.

Take a moment to think about what you really believe and notice what you are drawing into your life. What do you believe about yourself, about God, about money, about your job, about your family, about your friends, and about life in general? Review your beliefs to understand which energies you attract. If you impart negative thoughts to your energy field, you will attract events and people that manifest negative beliefs. Negative energy begets negative experience, which reinforces negative beliefs. Conversely, if you radiate positive beliefs and thoughts, you will draw the situations to you that confirm your beliefs and rein-force your positive life experience.

The advantage of positive thoughts is that they are electrically charged at a higher frequency than negative thoughts. They also extend out farther and with greater strength into the universe. They leave you with a feeling of expansiveness, growth, and lightness. Negative thoughts are dense and heavy, whereas positive thoughts are light and high in vibration. Observe people's body posture and you can get a sense of how these frequencies affect them physically. People who are self-confident usually hold themselves tall and upright, as though they could lift right off the ground. Their breathing is full and expands the lungs, chest, and abdomen. People with heavy and dense negative energy look as though they are carrying a heavy backpack at all times. Their shoulders are often rounded, their head tilts down, and their breathing is shallow as if there just is not any room for breath in their lungs. They often feel tightness and stress in the upper back and shoulders. The density of negative energy causes the body to collapse inwardly. Healing is the art and science of managing not only these energy fields, but also their root cause.

It is possible to feel the different nature of energies in another person. Try this experiment: Have the person think intense negative thoughts of self-loathing and poor self-worth. Place your hands above their head and try to feel the energy radiating out. You will have the impression of a collapsing, dense aura. Next, help the same person think strong positive thoughts of their importance and self-worth. You can literally feel the difference in the energy as it expands outward with lightness and happiness. When working with someone in this activity, remember to finish on the positive note.

Energy changes with intention, instantaneously and powerfully. Changing your electromagnetic field of energy is not difficult, nor does it take years of study or practice. It is immediate. You can understand this by simply changing your thoughts and noticing the instant shift in the energy within and around you. Through practice, you can better manage, moment to moment, the energy that surrounds you. Your work in self-discovery, digging deeply into your belief system and scrutinizing your core beliefs, will allow you to permanently intensify the positive energy you radiate and attract. You can project energies that contribute meaningfully to a better universe and a better life for all people.

All objects possess an energy field and radiate and attract energy. Energy can transfer and be shared between objects, creating a bond or magnetism. This energy exchange explains the phenomenon of dowsing rods, which have been used for thousands of years to locate sources of water. They are still used today by power companies, which employ them to locate water mains. This shared transfer and bonding of energy is also what psychics use to find missing objects or people.

In the case of a missing person, an article of clothing or jewelry provides an energy source, which connects to the missing person and allows the psychic to determine location. I have done many readings for people by holding a piece of their jewelry and intuitively reading their energy. I have received amazing information about their current condition, past experiences, health, and emotional problems.

The electromagnetic fields around both nonliving and living beings are active and moving, establishing connections from one form to another. A memory of attraction exists. The spirits taught me firsthand about this energetic attraction in a way I will never forget.

"Nothing Is Lost in God" was the title of a sermon I heard years ago in a Unity church. I loved the sermon, but the only thing I remembered explicitly was the title. I really liked the phrase, and it must have sunk deep into my memory bank. The concept reassured me and made me feel safe.

Several years ago, my family was visiting Sunriver, Oregon, a beautiful vacation spot in central Oregon in the high desert area. The resort where we stayed had many outdoor amenities that we loved. My husband was speaking at a convention, so the kids and I explored the resort on our own. We rented bicycles and took off for an outing along their bike trails. My oldest was seven and the twins were five, so when we came upon a giant playground we had to stop. We dismounted and carefully arranged the bikes so that we could lock them up safely. Each child wanted to be keeper of the keys, so I reluctantly separated the keys from the master key ring and divvied them up.

The playground was about 100 yards long with all kinds of wooden play equipment. There were swings, slides, climbing bars, and jungle gyms. The ground was covered in bark dust, several inches thick, creating a wonderful, cushioned landing spot—especially if you were five and performing your famous aerial dismount from the swing set. This was truly the perfect play spot. And play we did. We covered the entire area, climbing, sliding, running, chasing, competing, and having fun. Hours passed by.

When it was time to leave, we searched our pockets for bike keys only to realize one of them was lost. I despaired when I thought of the massive playground and its thick layer of bark dust.

My heart sank. "There is no way we will ever find it," I thought.

I immediately started figuring out how we could walk to the bike center, explain the situation, and hopefully get someone to cut off the bike lock. I wondered if the bike center had peanut butter sandwiches available because now I was also dealing with starving children who were not interested in delaying their lunch while we took care of this unexpected business. The situation was a bit nerve wracking.

Then a voice came into my head, "Nothing is lost in God."

I almost laughed out loud as I thought, "You have got to be kidding."

However, I found myself saying to the kids, "Well, let's give it a try and see if we can find the key."

We scouted the grounds for about ten minutes with absolutely no luck and I thought, "This is ridiculous; let's go."

Again the voice said, "Nothing is lost in God."

My mind flashed to the things the spirits had taught me about energy and attraction. I could feel the spirits' presence and their urging me to remember the laws, to trust, and to act. Spontaneously, I turned and threw the remaining key ring as hard as I could down the length of the playground. It traveled about fifty feet.

My kids looked at me with dumbfounded expressions and gasped, "What are you doing, Mom?"

Not wanting to explain the concept of the laws of attraction, I just said, "Oh, playing a game. I was just wondering if the key ring could find the key."

Being the ages they were, they thought this was great fun and ran toward the fallen key ring. We all strained our eyes, moving bark dust aside to no avail.

I eventually said, "Oh well, we tried," and I thought to myself, "at least I did not lose too much face."

I reached down to get the empty key ring. To all of our amazement, the key ring had landed on top of the missing key!

Even at the ages of five and seven, the children knew that a miracle had just happened. We all collapsed to the ground in amazement. The joy we felt was incredible. We were laughing and hugging and kissing each other. We were filled with glee. Spirit was so present, and we responded in a totally uninhibited way. We had observed a seemingly impossible situation change before our eyes—the laws of attraction had played themselves out.

After the excitement subsided, the kids asked, "How did that happen?"

We began a beautiful dialog. It was the perfect opportunity to talk about spirit and what we choose to believe. I told them of the voice that presented itself to me and what the spirits had taught me before. I explained that I had been presented with a choice. I had the choice to trust the voice or to ignore it. It was up to me to be willing and then to act on faith. Because of my actions, the miracle could manifest. How many times do we turn away from that small voice within and miss the miracle?

You must understand that I was dealing with very young children and they took this concept to the extreme. For the rest of the afternoon and night, our condo looked like the land of flying objects. The kids hid one shoe and threw the other to find it, or pants tried to find underwear, or socks looked for their mates. I had to duck a lot, but it was sure fun to watch them experiment and play this out in their own way.

As a result of this experience, I began to grasp the science behind the magical qualities of healing objects. Crystals contain powerful energy attracted from the earth in which they were formed. The compressed energy of the crystal operates at an extremely high frequency and purity. Because of the strong healing frequencies that crystals possess, they are often used in the healing arts. The energy they bring overcomes the low frequency—negative energy—that produced the wound or illness. The magnetic power of the individual's energy can draw to it the positive energy of the crystal, but one's mental attitude determines the degree of the attraction.

Sweat lodges, a Native American ceremony, have a great deal of energy attraction and exchange. The stones of the sweat lodge are heated by burning wood from trees. The energy of the tree is imparted to the stone, as is the energy of the water poured over the stones during the ceremony. The resultant steam contains the energy of the stones, the trees, and the water. As the steam fills the lodge, it radiates this energy into each participant. This is the source of the cleansing. The positive energy of the Earth Mother, in stone, tree, and water, flows into the human body to reconnect us with our origins and oneness with nature. One sits in the lodge on a dirt floor, in direct contact with the earth, to establish a link. The positive intention of participants in the lodge attracts the positive energy of the universe from all of these sources and makes us whole again.

Feathers, bones, teeth, and other remains of animals are imbued with the energy, which the animal possessed in life. The eagle feather carries the power of the eagle and, when used in ceremony, can impart this energy to the participants. In the same way, animal bones, teeth, hides, fur, and hair, even the earth on which they have trodden, contain remnants of the animals' energy. If we use these objects in a good way, we attract their power to ourselves. In many Native American and other indigenous cultures, hunters drink the blood or eat the heart of the animal they have killed to draw into himself or herself the animal's energy and to honor the power of its energy. The death of the animal, as with the death of a person, does not terminate the energy the animal radiated. It permeates everything within the concentric circles of the animal's aura.

Few of us today hunt animals and eat their hearts to merge with the animal, but eating any food does have an impact on your energy system. You still merge with the plant or animal. It still gives its life and energy to sustain yours. There is a sacred exchange of energy that should be honored and respected. It is important to pay attention to the foods you eat, to how they were grown, to the presence of toxins, and to the quality of energy they contain. The very spirit of the people and their relationship to the land can create an energy of love that is transferred to the food. The way people have treated the animals they raise is transferred to the animals, becoming part of the cumulative energy of the food we consume.

My family and I participated in a cooperative farm venture where families worked together to produce their food in a good way. Our work included harvest festivals and shared love. The foods we harvested were imbued with an aura of love and the energies of our shared work. Many have experienced this investment of energy at family gatherings where home cooked meals are a product of shared joy and love. The energy passes tangibly into the foods we prepare and consume, resulting in deep satisfaction. Not only is our hunger satisfied, but so is our soul as it emotionally connects to the energy of the food. Prayer said at mealtime adds energy to the food prior to consuming it. When food is prepared in a bad way, it brings an entirely different energy with it. It may cause indigestion or feelings of fullness without satisfying one's hunger.

Energy is a profound quality of life. It is everything and affects everything. At the beginning of the book, I referred to the soul as a composite of all the experiences ever had by an individual. Inanimate objects, plants, and animals also have collective experiences, which are housed in cellular memory. When you eat food, buy things, adorn your body, or decorate your home, you are subjected to this collective energy. Pay attention to what you bring into your life.

All beliefs and thoughts create the *electromagnetic* field
that surrounds you.

What are you attracting to yourself?

Collective Consciousness

What is meant by the term "collective consciousness?" It is a collection of thoughts shared by all beings that has as its source the oneness of the universe. Other terms for collective consciousness are "mass consciousness," "collected thought forms," or "universal consciousness."

Mass consciousness grows from energy—the energy that is accumulated from every thought or word spoken by every person. We all contribute. All thoughts are energy—powerful energy—and energy attracts like energy. Love attracts love; fear attracts fear. Remember that whatever you add energy to multiplies—it does not add, it multiplies. It multiplies because it grows not only from your own energy, but also from the contribution of what other people are thinking. This collection of thoughts creates a "collective consciousness." Every thought contributes to this pool, actually creating an energy form, which is otherwise known as a "thought form." The thought form is real—people who are attuned to and can see energy fields usually describe it as a cloudlike formation, varying in color and sometimes accompanied by a sound or smell.

A visual analogy of the creation of thought forms and their attraction of like forms is found in outer space. Have you ever seen pictures of astronauts in space trying to eat or drink? Because of the lack of gravity, liquids are covered so they do not float out of their containers. Imagine there are two astronauts trying to drink two juices—one grape and the other orange. They knock into one another, spilling their juices into the empty space of the cockpit. Since there is no gravity, the splash of juices separate into individual droplets and float around the cockpit. As the individual droplets float, they begin to merge with other droplets. Eventually a mass of juice floats in the cockpit, a puddle suspended in space. Amazingly, all of the grape juice droplets merge together and all of the orange juice droplets merge together, each attracted to their like and creating two complete puddles of juice. This is a visual representation of the *law of attraction*, the process by which energy is attracted to like energy.

Every thought you think or word you speak is like those individual droplets of juice. All float into space and go somewhere. The word and thought energies connect with similar thoughts and words. This collection of thought and word energy grows and grows as it is fed by more individuals' thoughts and words. This energy manifests and creates a reality of some sort. There are positive and negative realities created in this process. Fear, worry, hatred, greed, and dishonesty all create incredibly negative thought forms, with many people continually feeding them and contributing to their manifestation. We have examples of negative realities all over our planet.

Let me share some examples that may coincide with your own experiences and give you a more tangible connection with the concept of collective consciousness. Take a moment to think about some of the cities you have visited. Cities usually have a distinctive feel to them. You may have felt energized, nervous, scared, or enveloped in the history of a particular city you have visited.

I remember a client of mine saying, "I do not know what happened to me. I was driving on the highway in Los Angeles and I found myself honking my horn and flipping people off. That is just not like me. I have never acted like that before. It is totally against my principles." What happened? The collective consciousness lingering around that highway affected her. The accumulation of negative energy generated in that area by continual driving irritation, frustration, and rudeness entered her own consciousness, and she responded in a like manner.

Places hold collective consciousness in them. When you walk into buildings, they each have a "feel," especially the old ones. I was nearly brought to my knees when I walked into the Sistine Chapel in Italy. The magnificence of that place was truly overwhelming. I was only 22 years old, with absolutely no wisdom concerning spiritual matters, and had not entered looking for or expecting spiritual energy. Yet when I walked in, my knees started to buckle and I got goose bumps all over my entire body. I was awestruck. Millions of people had walked into that chapel before me and shared their awe, their prayers, and their love of God. The energy of those feelings lingers and grows. I had a very different experience when I visited the concentration camps in Germany. I cried uncontrollably. The terror, sadness, and depth of despair still linger there; it was a horrific experience. Although these are examples of two extremes in accumulated energies, they describe the phenomenon. All places have an energy to them—even your home or the individual rooms of your home. Become aware of what the energy of places feels like. As you tune in to these feelings and understand them in terms of energy, you enhance your work with energy.

Thought forms can control behavior and influence thinking because, knowingly or unknowingly, individuals tap into a collective consciousness, which actually exists. Even though you may not be able to see it, it is there. Remember, we are made of energy and are affected by the energy around us. Ideas, concepts, experiences, events, issues, cultures, and spiritual doctrines all have prevailing thought forms connected to them, which may represent hundreds of years of accumulated energy.

Thought forms follow the laws of energy. When you look at all-encompassing attitudes such as hatred, you can understand how massive some thought forms are and why they seem so impossible to heal. However, since all thought forms follow the laws of energy, it is entirely possible to change general attitudes and realities based in hatred or fear. Remember, manifestation comes about from an accumulation of energy. Thus, when you pray for global peace, visualize a healed planet, or speak of brotherly love. The energy of these actions has a powerful impact. Positive ideology and prayer adds positive energy to the collective consciousness, creating the possibility for hopeful change. The more people who add to this consciousness, the greater the likelihood for positive change.

You do not have to be on the front lines to make a difference. You are just as responsible for change as anybody else. My spirit helpers call this "praying behind the scenes." The prayers you contribute from your own home make a difference. Not everybody is a lobbyist or activist, but everyone does contribute by his or her thoughts and words. This is how we all are accountable. What do you manifest by your thoughts for yourself, your schools, your communities, and your nation? Which thought forms do you add energy to—positive hope and healing or continuous complaint? Watch out. Part of the responsibility for being awake and conscious requires the monitoring of your own thoughts.

Walking the spiritual path is having an understanding of the impact of your energy and its contribution to the universe. Healers, masters, psychics, and inventors tap into thought forms to acquire information. Some are doing this consciously and some unknowingly, but the result is that they get information that can be of service to them. The shamanic journey and meditation are both excellent methods for energy reading. Remember, thoughts are energy, and they contain information. Learning to read this information can be extremely helpful both for yourself and for others. You can literally pull information and guidance to yourself by speaking your intention, stilling your mind, and then allowing the guidance to merge with your intention. Everyone can develop these skills with practice and dedication, which, in turn, opens an infinite variety of doors to greater understanding.

Creating Change:
Practical Application of the Laws of Energy

Now that you understand some of the basic laws of energy, let's look at some of the ways they can be applied to your everyday life. Spirit continually tells me that humans have an incredible power to create. In fact, you create your reality every moment by the way you think, speak, and act. You also create your reality from your belief system—what you believe about yourself, about individual things, about concepts such as prayer, and what you believe about Creator. All will have a profound effect on you and what you create in your life. You also have full power to change any of the beliefs that are not servicing you. You can direct energy in such a way that you manifest your heart's desires. Albert Einstein stated, "We cannot solve the problems of today at the level of thinking we were at when we created them." We create reality by our thoughts, and only by a redirection of our thoughts are we able to move into a new reality.

Visualization

Visualization is a foundational tool for use in manifesting your desires. It can be extremely helpful in gaining clarity about yourself, your core beliefs, and what you truly are seeking in your life. Many people do not know what they really want from life. Clarity is necessary before change is possible. Visualization also helps develop a solid prayer life. In fact, visualization is actually a powerful form of prayer.

Visualization is based on the laws of energy. If you add energy to a thought by continually thinking about it, you start the process of creation. Physical reality can be created by continued thought, imagination, planning, designing, and focused energy.

One way of practicing visualization is to create a goal board. Goal boards are visual and physical prayers. Remember that prayers are concentrated, focused energy directed to a Force greater than self. With goal boards, you create a physical representation of your goals and a visual focal point to your prayers.

Goal boards can be as simple as a collage of pictures on a large poster board. The pictures represent what you hope, wish, and intend to manifest. You can have many requests on one board. Simply cut out pictures from magazines, sketch pictures, or write out prayers in simple sentences and paste them on poster board. Written statements by the pictures will reinforce that particular goal.

For example, if you want a new car and are not in a position to walk into a dealership and purchase one, you could decide to apply the theory of visualization. Create a goal board. Cover it with pictures of the car you seek. Write out your wish in a confirmed statement. For example, "Thank you for the divine car." Think positively, and visualize the wish fulfilled. Color, texture, creativity, and expressions of self all create a fun and a powerful goal board. With every magazine you search through, each picture you cut out, every drop of creativity used, you are actually directing energy toward your goal. Throughout the entire process, your intention is focused on your goal, and in turn, your goal accumulates energy.

Once you have completed your goal board, you visualize with it or meditate with it every day. Each day you look at the cut-out pictures of this new car; you *see* yourself driving it, *feel* your body sitting inside, *hear* the engine start up, *smell* the new interior. You use all of your senses to engage in the fact that you own this car. This process actually magnifies the energy of creation. Place the goal board in a room you frequent throughout the day; then every time you see your goal board, send energy to your goal. This serves as a great reminder to focus your thoughts.

You might go to a car dealership and test drive the car you desire so that you can experience it on an emotional and physical level. All actions add energy to the fact that you own the car. Concentrated attention is how we manifest. The mind becomes focused and the energy multiplies, until the energy manifests in physical form. Visualization works. Companies have studied its use to create and market products; athletes have used it to improve their performance.

My Personal Success with Visualization

My own personal experience with visualization changed my life. I had a deep longing to move to the Northwest many years before I actually did. I had known the Northwest only through pictures and movies. However, its beauty had captivated my interest, and I could feel the place calling to me. I wondered why I felt such strong connections to a place I had never been. As I privately contemplated these internal nudges to relocate, I held my thoughts to myself. My best friend later moved to Portland, Oregon, which then provided me with incentive to visit this mystery place of my subconscious. After just one visit, I fell in love with the mountains, the rivers, and the trees, and my soul connected in a way that felt like home. I knew this was where I wanted to live. I started to pray, asking for divine intervention and open doors of opportunity.

I told my husband I wanted to move to Oregon. He was extremely supportive, honoring my desire, but also apprehensive of job opportunities and how we would sustain ourselves if we moved. We were living in Texas at the time, and both of us worked in education. His concerns were normal—the distance of the move, moving expenses, the availability of jobs, and the likelihood of being hired for an administrative position from out of state. I, on the other hand, paid no attention to these concerns and became dazzled with creating dreams of our relocation. As soon as I knew that I had my husband's support and willingness to move, all systems were "Go, Go, Go." I believed that all things were possible, and instead of worrying about the obstacles; I concentrated on what I wanted and created my dream.

I placed pictures of Oregon on my desk at work. Every time I looked up from my paperwork, I saw the landscape of this beautiful state. I took a few moments to envision myself there, hiking on the mountain trails, walking along the beach, visiting with my best friend. At home I constructed a goal board I meditated with every day. The goal board consisted of pictures and written prayers. I had pictures of what I imagined to be the divine educational setting, perfect house, a moving van, and a "For Sale" sign outside our Texas home. The board was full of things that indicated a move into a divine situation, with everybody happy. We are a family of five, so I had a lot of people to consider while I created at my heart's desire.

I started my goal board in November. In March, we decided to travel to Oregon for spring vacation, just to look around. The likelihood of job interviews was slim because Portland schools were also on spring break, and we had made few preliminary arrangements. Using the phone book, my husband had already sent resumes to area districts. We arrived on a Saturday and he began calling districts on Monday, hoping to get an initial interview. He hoped for a follow-up interview on a return trip. Most districts were not hiring or had already selected their primary candidates for administrative positions.

One of the districts informed my husband that five finalists had already been selected and final interviews scheduled, but that he could meet with the personnel director the next day. Meanwhile, the personnel director shared my husband's resume with the superintendent, who suggested that he be added to Wednesday's interview schedule. By the time my husband returned to our hotel, he had received a telephone message giving him an interview time. The interview committee was so impressed with him, the next day, that the superintendent called afterward to request a breakfast meeting. Early Friday morning, my husband was offered the job.

Signs of other forces at work accompanied the whirlwind of events and their sudden culmination in a successful job offer. While I waited in the parking lot, during my husband's initial interview, I asked for a sign that the move to the Northwest was right—a part of the divine order of our lives and not merely a whim that had taken over my psyche. I was asking my family to commit to huge changes and now, at this last hour, I called out to Spirit in desperation. "Show me a sign that this is right; signal me by the appearance of a hawk."

Almost immediately, I saw a distant speck on the horizon of an approaching bird, and then another. At first I suspected they might be local buzzards, and I was concerned about the possible meaning of such a sign. But as they drew near I recognized them as red-tailed hawks. Excitedly, I left the car to watch them fly in circles above me. They joined in a love tryst in the air and tumbled down in a love grip. Intimate, sacred, and oh so blatant! I knew this was a positive omen of divine intervention. With tears rolling down my face, I said thank you to the universe. I knew before my husband did that he had been chosen for the position. I watched the rest of the process throughout the week with a smile of knowingness.

We left Oregon that spring-break week with my husband securing the job of his dreams. There was a divine match in philosophies and personalities between him and the school district's administrative staff. The new school district even offered to pay our moving expenses! It seemed that all of our major concerns were addressed and eliminated. We returned home, put our house on the market, and moved by June. The improbable happened with no worry and no anxiety, just focused attention dedication to the process, and the belief that all things are possible through prayer.

We decided to live in an apartment for our first year in Portland so we could make a quality decision about where to buy our "dream house." I kept saying it needed to be perfect. This would be the house where my children would grow up—the neighborhood where they would establish their roots. It was very important to me.

I again created a goal board. I cut out pictures of happy kids with big smiles and sparkling eyes, having fun. I placed pictures of my own children in the middle of all these pictures. I did not notice it until later but several of the pictures I had cut out were of Japanese/American children.

I also wrote out 34 things I wanted in a house; I was extremely specific. I visualized the house, the neighborhood, and the community atmosphere. I imagined the sounds, colors, textures, and smells, stimulating all of my senses to the greatest degree. I held fast to my desires even though there were several obstacles, mostly financial, to being able to afford the house I visualized. It took one year for the whole thing to manifest, but when it did it was ideal. We found the house we desired, with almost every detail created. In fact, 32 of the 34 specifics were obvious manifestations of my dream. The house was absolutely perfect, and yes, as it turned out, the neighborhood was full of happy kids—five of them being Japanese/American!

As we stood in the driveway, excited about finding our home, hawks circled overhead from the woods behind the house. Perhaps the same hawks, perhaps not, but certainly the same message.

At their arrival, my husband said to me, "It's a done deal, isn't it?"

"There's the sign," I replied pointing to the sky.

The hawks had confirmed our decision. To this day, the hawk has remained an important sign of confirmation for me.

The results of visualization can be extremely accurate, so you want to be as specific with your focused energy as possible. You manifest what you concentrate on, so be clear and precise in your prayers. If you become discouraged, frustrated, or wishy-washy, you may cancel your own prayers. Remember, prayer is energy, focused and directed toward the manifestation of something you desire. Discouragement and frustration are also energy. If you spend several hours a day entertaining negative attitudes, they will then grow and gain more power than your original prayer. *Whatever gets the greater energy wins!* Get clear about what you want and then hold true to your desire. Doubt is energy that will create more doubt.

Throughout the selling of our house in Texas and the purchase of our home in Oregon, my specific prayer was that a divine situation be created for *all concerned.* The results were positive. Even the seemingly disappointing one-year delay in the sale of our house in Texas turned out to be positive. The wait resulted in our buying the house we wanted, which went on the market the week we closed our house in Texas. If such had not been the case, we might have settled for less. The spirits acted to provide the right opportunity at the right moment. They also provided me with a wonderful teaching not to be discouraged when my desires do not manifest immediately. There is a reason for the delay. My gains in understanding the importance of trust, faith, and focused attention were part of the payoff. A win-win attitude keeps energy flowing in a clear and open way.

The real gift of this work is mastering the process of creating. Remember, you cannot *not* be creating; you are creating with every thought you have. Visualization through the goal board focuses your thoughts and your feelings. Once you master this type of focused attention, you can apply it to any part of your life. Learning to create abundance is a process of growth, empowerment, developing worth, and connection to Spirit. The process of visualization helps define your relationship to Spirit in a very tangible way. I always include a section on my board just for thanksgiving. Although this is not necessary in creating a goal board, it will remind you that the goal board is a form of connection with spirit.

Once your goal board has worked its magic, disassemble it with an attitude of gratitude. Spirit is connected to this goal board, for it holds many prayers.

Daydreaming is a form of visualization in which you literally hold your dream fondly in the back of your mind, and spontaneously add positive thought and energy to it. Stop for a moment and think about something you really wanted in the past that you actually received. Focus on your thoughts and your imagination. You were probably clear about what you really wanted. When you look back, you might notice that you had actually been thinking about that desire for years. Recall how much energy you put into the end result, probably in the form of daydreaming. Daydreaming is wonderful because it uses the imagination and declares anything is possible. Daydreaming is clear of doubt, and is a pure vision of success!

Take a moment to think about people you know who seem able to manifest quickly. What do you notice about them? A main characteristic is trust. They have an unshakeable trust in themselves and in the universe, which builds confidence in their abilities to create. However, most people are not that pure with their thinking. They contaminate their thoughts with doubts. They might really want a car and go through the whole process of visualization, and then completely sabotage their goal with doubts and fears.

Typical doubts and fears have to do with worth. Am I really deserving of a car like this? Is it proper to ask for such a materialistic item? Many people start to doubt their ability to come up with the down payment. They might see themselves gaining a new car but losing someplace else in their life because of large monthly payments. They might see the bank refusing their loan or doubt that the car is really the best choice.

All of these thoughts are energy too. They are based in fear, doubt, and a sense of unworthiness. Such thoughts impact the underlying belief systems of many people. They become huge thought forms and manifest easily because there is so much energy continually directed toward them. *Whatever you add the most energy to will manifest.* You can easily cancel or neutralize your goal/prayer by doubtful thoughts. Or worse, you can manifest your doubts and fears. When fear and doubt consume more of your thought processes than do your dreams and desires, your fears and doubts will tip the balance. The choice is always yours. Where is your energy going? What are your underlying beliefs about manifestation? Think about what you are thinking…

If you do not get the results you want immediately, do not give up and assume it was not meant to be. Do not replace your positive energy with negative. Detach from what you are trying to create and let the timing be. Remember back to your daydreaming when you most likely relished in the fantasy of your heart's desire without attaching a time schedule. So often, when you let the universe fulfill your prayers in its own time, the end result is even better than you had imagined.

Remember to trust and understand that what you put energy toward will manifest. Continually remind yourself that you are a co-creator in this beautiful universe and that your thoughts are powerful. I purposefully chose the example of a car because, as such a materialistic item, it may push lots of "belief system buttons" for individual readers. Materialism is not the best motivation for directing energy, but the example presses the point that all thoughts are energy and all thoughts impact outcomes, material or otherwise.

Look closely at your beliefs and again evaluate where they come from. This is all part of the bigger picture of self-discovery and will help you identify your blocks to manifestation. Experiment with visualization, practice it, and pay attention to the results. It can help build faith as well as self-awareness.

Affirmations and Mantras

Affirmations and mantras are statements you say to yourself in a repetitive and rote way. Affirmations have been used in psychology for years as part of the healing process for clients, with varying degrees of success. Mantras have been used for thousands of years by monks to train their mind. Both affirmations and mantras are methods of focused attention and concentration. Their success is based on the number of repetitions and the level of commitment to the process. Which do you think have been more successful, the psychology clients or the monks?

The spirits taught me about the power of affirmations and mantras as I was doing soul retrievals for people. Whenever I finished a journey, the spirits would assign a mantra for my client to repeat. I was to give my client the mantra, with instructions to repeat it a specific number of times first thing in the morning for 60-90 days. Then one day the spirits instructed me to tell a particular client to say a mantra for ten days, 560 times per day. I was shocked. The number of repetitions was staggering to me. The spirits informed me that this process was a necessary component to enhance the healing my client had just received. From then on, the spirits continued to assign mantras to my clients, but with large numbers of repetitions.

The spirits never let me off the hook, so they gave me a mantra to practice also. I diligently sat every day repeating my phrase; it took me about an hour each day. To my amazement it had a tremendous impact on me. The practice became rote and, in fact, a part of my being. Because of the repetitions, the mantra became embedded in my psyche like a catchy tune. Then a magical truth was created and revealed; the mantra stayed in my mind and eventually created a new *core* to my belief system. Days turned into months and years, and I now have a hard time even remembering the faulty belief system that caused me so much pain in the past. Remember that you respond from a belief system with every choice, thought, or action you have; this is an automatic response. When you want to experience permanent change, you need to address your belief system.

The spirits informed me that the purpose of a mantra is to change the patterning of the mind. The mind is rarely still. It has a background chatter, often referred to as "self-talk," that is activated (probably even as you are reading this). In many cases, self-talk is destructive. It becomes your own personal berating system. Your early belief system may have been put into place years before and it takes much effort to reprogram it. Saying an affirmation a few times a day, even if it is for three months, probably will not have much effect. But anything that you say 500-600 times a day will. You will find yourself saying it while you wash your hair, do the dishes, and drive the car. It becomes the new self-talk—the new background noise.

Spiritual initiates have known the power of mantras for eons; religious doctrines are based on this concept. Prayer beads and rosaries are simple counting systems for repetitive statements. Initiates sit for hours, days, and years chanting mantras and programming their minds with spiritual doctrines. This ancient method works.

I prefer using a clock. I notice how long it takes to say the mantra the initial time and then multiply that out to determine the total time needed. In that way, I do not need to keep an exact count and I know that when I have completed the time, I will have said the mantra the required repetitions. I also do not have to think about manipulating my prayer beads, but can focus on my mantra. Whichever method you decide on, prayer beads or timing, this process takes a tremendous commitment. However, the pay off is that progress is fast. If you dedicate just ten days to 600 daily repetitions, you will experience an amazing difference in your self-talk. The more you practice, the faster the transformation will take place. It can be done formally, sitting in front of an altar, or informally, while you are doing other activities. I made a pact with myself that I would not listen to the radio anymore in the car, and that no matter where I was going I would say my mantra the entire way. It was amazing how wonderful I felt, when I arrived at my destination, and the magic that followed. I had built up positive energy along the way, and the energy hovered around me for hours afterward. I might find incredible deals if I were shopping or find a parking place in crowded parking lots or have great interactions with people. It was like I was charmed.

You may put your mantra or affirmation to music and sing your tune throughout the day. Pick a jingle that sticks with you and plug in the words. Music has a profound effect on the psyche and is a wonderful way to memorize. Just think of it—can you imagine trying to learn the alphabet without singing the alphabet song?

Creating mantras or affirmations for yourself is easy, but there are a few rules that should be followed. Keep the mantras positive and somewhat short. Negative words such as *not, don't, won't*, for example, are not recognized by the subconscious mind and should be avoided. "I love myself," has greater impact than, "I don't hate myself anymore."

I will list several mantras the spirits have given my clients along with ones I have accumulated over my years of study. Trudy Bragg, my hypnosis teacher, contributed many.

One of my favorites is an ancient Tibetan mantra:

> May I be filled with loving kindness,
> May I be well,
> May I be peaceful and at ease.
> May I be happy.

I especially like to say this one as I am gardening; it has such a grounding effect on me.

Another favorite of mine is a song I learned in the Unity church:

> I am walking in the light, in the light, in the light.
> I am walking in the light, in the light of God.

This is the one I sing in the car, and I can feel the light energy build around me. It has a catchy tune that stays with me.

Other possible mantras are:

- I am whole. I am happy. My life reflects the splendor of the universe.

- I accept, honor, and respect all parts of myself.

- I am whole. I am happy, and each and every day I release more of my pain, anger, and unforgiveness.

- I love myself; I am a worthy person.

- I treat myself with the greatest of respect.

- Thank you, Great Spirit, for the increased growth and insight into the spiritual realm.

- I am one with Great Spirit.

- I am success; I am unlimited.

- Thank you, Great Spirit, for our divine marriage; it grows in love and respect each day.

- Thank you, Great Spirit, for the divine love in our family; we all treat each other with integrity and respect.

- Thank you, Great Spirit, for laughter each day.

- Thank you, Great Spirit, for divine spiritual growth and understanding.

- I have found heaven on earth.

- Thank you, Great Spirit that my meditations and journeys are direct links into the spiritual realm. I am growing in my awareness each and every day.

- Thank you, Great Spirit, for open doors of opportunity; all doors are open and I easily connect to my divine path.[1]

- Thank you, Great Spirit, for the divine solution to this situation.[2]

- Thank you, Great Spirit, for the healing in my life; I am divinely healed.[3]

- Thank you, Great Spirit, wherever I go I shall meet with friendship and love.[4]

- Thank you, Great Spirit, for abundant money. I have much to give.[5]

- The universe responds to me and I create my heart's desires.[6]

- The spirit in me forgives and sends love to you. I am free.[7]

- Divine love is doing its perfect work in me and through me now.[8]

- Divine love brings into my life the right people. Those people who are not for my highest good now fade out of my life and find their good elsewhere. I walk in the charmed circle of God's love.[9]

- I am divinely led to say the right thing, at the right time. All doors are open to me now, professionally, personally, and emotionally.[10]

- I have many good and trusting friends. I bring only good into my life. Thank you.

- I am prosperous now in love and money.[11]

- There is nothing to fear. Anything in my life that needs to be changed can be changed.[12]

- I call unto myself only divine solutions.

> Try this powerful mantra for yourself, and say it 200 times a day:
> I am open to receive the splendors of the universe.

The spirits told me to quit praying for healing and to start claiming: *I am healed*

Monitoring Your Thoughts

Every thought you have is either creating positive or negative influences in your life. This is where our accountability and responsibility as a co-creator with Creator gets very personal. No one can climb into your head and monitor your thinking—plus, you could always say one thing but be thinking another! The only one who knows the truth is you!

You are always thinking. The mind never takes a rest. If left to wander, the mind would be creating all sorts of scenarios, remembering incidents in full detail, replaying conversations, and, worst of all, berating self at every opportunity. This mind activity controls your emotions, feelings, attitude, heartbeat, and ultimately how you feel about yourself. You may think of an incident that happened twenty years ago and suddenly become completely depressed. You may react emotionally, mentally, and physically by recalling a long-suppressed memory. You thus become a victim of your thoughts—not a victim of the actual incident, but of your mind. Most thinking patterns are habits. I have seen many people receive healings, but then lose the effects of those healings by falling back into old patterns of habitual thoughts (usually thoughts stemming from feelings of unworthiness or not loving self). Getting control of the mind will take some practice, but it can be done. If you learn to monitor and modify your thoughts, your life will become enriched and transformed.

When you first begin to monitor your mind, you will likely feel overwhelmed. It is a huge task. But as you continually pay attention to what you are thinking, with intention and determination, it can be done. Keep encouraging yourself; the payoff from this type of control is phenomenal.

In most cases, mind monitoring fails because people literally forget to monitor. They get caught up in their day and forget all about the commitment to monitor their thoughts. There are so many demands, responsibilities, and general busyness throughout the day. With traffic, work schedules, the phone, housework, children, and errands, people are part of many routines.

Whatever your responsibilities, trying to change habitual, destructive thinking patters will be difficult. To valiantly say, "I have control of my thoughts; I choose to think positively," is the first step in the process of monitoring.

The second step is to actually start the process of monitoring. You need to establish some sort of reminder to yourself of the commitment you have made. Notes work well. If you are home during the day, try putting notes around the house—in the kitchen, the bathroom, cupboards, on or in the refrigerator, on the telephone. If you work in an office, place notes around your workspace, especially by the telephone and atop your desk. Put reminders inside your car or your lunch sack. Write reminders that make sense to you: *What am I thinking? Get control! I choose to think good thoughts.* Choose whatever words will remind you to tune into your thoughts and to take control of your mind.

Monitor your spoken words too. Words are power-packed with energy and create much faster than thoughts. How do you describe yourself during the day? How do you speak about your life, your job, and your life situations? Pay close attention to what you are affirming! If you are not satisfied with what you are say-ing, change it.

Another reminder idea is to take a small piece of folded paper and place it under your ring or your watch. You will continually feel the paper and be reminded of your commitment. The more you are reminded, the faster you will gain control. If none of these suggestions works for you, find something that will. Be creative, but remember this is a choice. Do not get down on yourself if you do not progress as quickly as you would like. You do not want to add negative energy to self-critical opinions you might already possess. Be gentle with yourself; the whole process takes time and effort. As the English poet Samuel Butler wrote, "Life is like playing a violin solo in public and learning the instrument as one goes on."

Detachment Provides a Clearer Perspective

All people are going to have experiences in their lives that they are emotionally attached to. Whenever this happens, it is difficult to get a true perspective on what to do. There is real truth in the saying, "Sometimes you cannot see the for-est for the trees." We are so involved in the immediate events of our lives, that we have difficulty perceiving its larger meaning. However, there are methods that can be used in all situations to help you detach from the emotions that cloud your vision.

1. One practical method of detachment is to write the situation on paper and then list the pros and cons. Even though this method seems simple, it has profound results. In the process of writing, your thoughts become organized. They move from random, scattered, and conflicting thoughts connected to abstract, dysfunctional scenarios into logical, rational sentences on paper. Also, when things are written, they have a different impact on the mind. A more black-and-white reality develops. The divided list makes it easier to see which set outweighs the other when you have divided views. Once you develop a list, keep it out in full view and review it regularly. It will enhance your ability to keep things in perspective.

2. Another way to detach from interfering emotions is to recreate the situation in third-person terms. Ask yourself what you would say to a friend who came to you with the same circumstances. Remove the emotions that you feel and simply look at the issues. Actually speak out loud, as though you were advis-ing this friend. When the mind is forced to form words, written or verbal, it

has to organize its thoughts and, in so doing, brings clarity to the generally disorganized randomness of the mind.

3.   Having a tool with which to analyze the situation is helpful. Remember, you are emotionally tied to a situation because of your belief systems. By detaching emotionally, you can better survey your belief system. The trick to discovering your true belief system is to work backwards from your reaction. Writing helps you to notice patterns in your thinking and behaviors. Write the following:

> how you feel
> how you act
> what you say
> what you think
> what you really believe (Always end on the question about belief.)

When your perceptions are clouded by conflicting emotions, detachment is difficult. In this case, it is helpful to become analytical and to describe the emotion in writing, using the same format as described above. A good example is anger:

> When I *feel* anger, I get hot, my body perspires, and I feel sensations up my spine.
> My *actions* are to yell, display a shortness of temper, and to not listen.
> I *say* things that are blaming and humiliating to another person. I say things that will cut them down and hurt them.
> I am *thinking* that I need to win, that I am being taken advantage of, and that I am not being heard.
> I *believe* that this other person is not seeing my worth. I believe that if they win, I will lose and that will make me a loser. Being a loser is what my father used to say to me and that causes me much pain. That pain hurts. So the belief that I develop is that I am not valued, and I feel worthless about myself, especially when I think I am not being heard.

This process of analysis takes time, but it works wonders. If you are diligent in writing out your responses in simple, clear-cut answers, you will notice amazing patterns in your thinking and behaviors. If you make the answers too long and complicated, finding the patterns will be more difficult.

The experiences in life you are emotionally linked to will be your greatest teachers for self-examination. Another common example of a conflicting emotion is fear around money and not having enough.

How you feel: "I get an upset stomach. I feel nervous and edgy. I feel resentful."

How you act: "I close down, I find myself turning away from activities and people."

What you say: "I cannot afford it. I do not have any money. Things are tough right now."

What you think: "I think that I never have enough, that everyone has more than I do, that money is a constant problem in my life. I will never get ahead and be able to do the things I enjoy."

What you really believe: "I believe that all of this manifestation stuff is hogwash. It doesn't really work for me. I'm not good enough. The people that this works for are better than I am."

A Worksheet in Problem Solving

How does the problem impact your life?
What does it cause you to do or not to do?
How does having the problem help in some way? What way?
How does it affect others?
-your spouse or life partner
-your children
-your mother
-your father
-your siblings
-your employer
-your coworkers
-your neighbors
-your friends
How does it affect your relationship with them?
If you could snap your fingers and get rid of the problem, how would your life be different?
Why are you not capable of releasing yourself from this problem with the snap of your fingers?
Do you recognize your body's response to the problem?
What is your emotional response?
What does your problem look like in light of what you believe about who you truly are?

You need to be very clear about your belief systems concerning the subject. If some of your responses seem immature, examine them more closely. Save your responses. Return to them when you have traveled further on your spiritual journey. Answer the questions again. Look to see how you have changed your perspective. Even when the problem remains the same, it will change inside of you and you will find that the problem is governed by your choices.

If you apply what you have learned about energy and belief systems, you will have a new perspective on how to create your own well being. You will strive for detachment and clarity so you can make quality decisions about your personal growth and enlightenment. You will understand that the element of choice is always present. Some behaviors will seem simple to change and others might require assistance. You may redefine some issues by simply deciding to change your belief system. In some cases, more intensive work with soul retrievals may be in order. In all cases, you want to bring Spirit into the situation. Ask for clarity, discernment, and the opening of the heart. This prayer brings light and positive energy to your situation. Think about the concept of love, which brings greater clarity to all understanding. All life experiences are rooted in love and growth. Remember this and utilize it in decision making. In this process of healing yourself, or becoming a better healer for others, your belief system will be continually challenged.

Thinking Differently

William James wrote, "Genius means little more than the faculty of perceiving in an unhabitual way." Our habits of thought often prevent us from considering other possibilities. Enlightenment and awareness are about change, including the change that comes to your thinking. Progress along the spiritual path is discovered in self-reflection, and changes are the guideposts. When you know yourself and are able to see the subtle changes in your being, as they occur—when you know you are different, and when you understand that you have changed, then you have advanced along the path.

The goal of the spiritual path is to learn to live in love, step away from judgments, be filled with trust and faith, and choose consistently the highest good for all.

Scrutinize your actions and thoughts. Are they based in fear or love? Love allows for growth, expansion, imagination, creation, support, trust, freedom, compassion, and possibilities. Fear encases one in competition, close-mindedness, self-indulgence, greed, arrogance, judgments, punishment, and attitudes of righ-teousness, dominance, jealousy, and feelings of unworthiness. Every thought, word, or action has its basis in one of these two feelings: fear or love. Remember that thoughts, words, and actions involve choice. Choose love; practice love.

The Role of Prayer in Change

One of the practices of love is prayer. Prayer should be a conscious part of the entire day. Formalized prayer is good, but informal prayer can become a natural part of one's daily way of being. It is the act of sending light, healing energy, and love from yourself into to all people and situations you encounter. No event is too minor for your healing prayers.

While watching the news, reading the paper, driving your car, doing your work, or shopping in the grocery store, bless those around you throughout the day. Consider each situation you come into contact with as needing your pro-jected love. These prayers and blessings are important to the world, to the people who surround you, and to yourself. Prayers come wrapped in compassion, not judgment; hence, they heal rather than hurt.

Years ago, I found myself in a terrible situation with a coworker who turned her turbulent, angry feelings toward me and set out to destroy my reputation. She sought vengeance for a situation for which I was not to blame. It started when I was invited to her engagement party. When I arrived, I met her fiancée, who rec-ognized me as his former high school biology teacher. He had been a rowdy, loud, and self-confident football player who had a high school crush on me. I was unaware of this (in fact, I barely remembered him), but as the night wore on and he drank more alcohol, his high school crush became magnified and boisterously broadcasted. He described in detail his heart yearnings for his high school teacher. I was extremely embarrassed. His fiancée, my coworker, became furious. Thus began her war against me.

The anger and humiliation she felt festered. She brought her angry energy to our workplace. It grew like the destructive thunderhead of an impending storm, black and heavy with explosive potential. She vented her hostility toward me. She was obviously in excruciating pain, as I understand now, but at the time I simply experienced a change in her behavior that was rude and vindictive. She attacked everything about me—my working skills, my personality, my integrity, even the way I dressed. There was nothing that I could do "right."

I became distressed. I started doubting myself and became consumed with the situation. It was taking a huge toll on my energy, affecting all facets of my life. I found myself shutting down. My job, my personality, my family, and my friends were all affected. I was hurting.

This experience happened early in my spiritual journey. I had very little real experience as to how Spirit worked. I had no knowledge of energy or the laws of manifestation. I just cried out in desperation to God. I knew I was no match for this woman and her deceit. I knew I could not fight fire with fire (although I was receiving advice to do so), so I decided to follow my heart. I made my decision from pure desperation. I started getting up about 4:30 every morning and praying for her and the situation. I knew that rage, vindictiveness, jealously, and aggression were all signs of deep pain. I tried to disconnect myself from being her victim and prayed for her healing. I visualized her a happy person and called forth great things to come her way. Since I did not know her personally, I simply enveloped her in light. I visualized it breaking through a tough, ugly, hostile exterior and filling her with soft, beautiful, loving light. I did the same for myself.

This went on for months. I chose to think positively, to immerse myself in my work, to close my office door, and to surround myself in peace. I would not engage in any conflict, I would not think negatively of the situation, and I spoke only loving words about her.

The news came one day that she would be leaving. She had taken a difficult licensing exam, passed it with flying colors, and was off to seek her fortune. That same month, I was awarded a prestigious award for the work I had just completed, which brought positive recognition to me and to my place of employment.

I was amazed at the turn of events. It was a win-win situation for everybody. After she left, the atmosphere around my job was light, joyful, and full of love and support. My home life changed, my relationship with my friends changed, I changed.

I experienced the remarkable glory of love and was in awe of how Spirit worked. I grasped the meaning of turning the other cheek. I had always thought it implied a loss of individual power. Now I realized that turning the other cheek could empower me. I was making energy work for me instead of against me. And it was done using the greatest force of the universe—love. I had activated my sacred choice of free will in dealing with the situation and had learned how to direct energy in a potent and productive way.

This experience was a huge step forward in my spiritual growth. I shudder to think what would have happened had I chosen to fight fire with fire. Or, if by feeling broken, confused, attacked and damaged, I had chosen to quit my job. The effects could have been devastating for years to come.

Instead, I chose to take care of myself in a healthy way. My thoughts, words, and actions all focused toward a positive outcome. Thought, word, and action manifested into reality. I learned that positive or negative choice is always present, and it is up to me to determine which attitude to bring to any given situation.

I have used this story many times while working with clients who are having difficulty with workplace dynamics. The outcome has been consistently positive. Thinking kindly of adversaries is not easy in the heat of the moment, but you need positive energy the most at that time. Ironically, the best way to deal with your aggressors is to love them.

Even if you took the component of love out of this story and focused upon the laws of energy (remembering that whatever you add energy to multiplies), the results of this teaching would be the same.

Try this process for yourself if you are ever in a relationship that you would like to heal. You will find the results to be truly amazing. Pay attention to the energy and what happens. Write the daily shifts you experience so that you can remember them clearly. Ask yourself: Where is my energy going? What am I thinking about in lieu of this situation? What am I saying? Your questions will add clarity, and you will learn to predict what form of manifestation is likely to occur based on the answers.

Prayer is a behind-the-scenes activity. It has both dramatic immediacy and subtle accumulation. Prayer is a powerful healer—the most powerful energy that exists. Use it for the good of all and you will receive bountifully.

Compassion

Have compassion for yourself and for others. Realize that life offers experiences, but it is often our judgments (of good, bad, right, or wrong) that hide the actual value of the experience. When you practice compassion, judgments have permission to fade away and greater growth is possible.

Compassion is love held in nonjudgment. It is the realization of another person's pain, and the profound understanding of the damage that suffering can cause. It is the ability to stand in the shoes of another person and to feel life as he or she feels it. It is a way of extending great care and love to another.

Emotional pain is a valid experience, a part of the human experience. The soul unfolds and develops in all experiences, including the ones that are painful. Understanding this is compassion.

Challenge Your Judgments; Increase Your Compassion

Difficult situations offer meaningful challenge but ultimately can strengthen the individual on a spiritual path. True compassion, true nonjudgment, is difficult, at best, but most difficult when applying it to a despicable person or situation. Think of the nightly news and the terrible crimes you have heard about. In such events, your nonjudgment can truly be challenged. Practice praying for the situation without judgment and allowing yourself to see the crime from all perspectives. First, become the victim and try to feel the energy of being a victim. Then become the perpetrator of the crime and feel that particular energy. Try to understand and to know the kinds of energy experienced by both victim and perpetrator.

If a weapon was used, become the weapon. Understand its energy. Feel the energy associated with the families of both the victim and the criminal as a result of this situation. Consider the reporter who investigated and wrote the story, the law enforcement officers, the juries, the judges, and the witnesses who might have been associated with the crime. Consider the physical location of the crime and the surrounding environment. Know the energy of the place as a result of the crime. Consider what has been absorbed into the landscape and the surroundings. Feel the dynamics of the entire situation. Understand without judgment, but feel deeply. Allow your heart to open and pray. Bring light and love to the incident and to all associated with it. Your mission is to send light and positive energy. Practice this every day.

The purpose of a daily effort to pray without judgment is two-fold. The energy you send forth alters all that it touches, and the act of praying alters you. You may never know the impact of your prayers on others, but you will see significant changes in yourself. You become your prayers. Prayers offered in compassion and love does change the world for the better, affecting both the recipients and the giver of the prayer. As we project love, so we receive love.

You will find that your heart automatically opens. Your capacity for compassion and love grows, as does your movement away from judgment of others. You will become less likely to "cast the first stone." You contribute yourself to a growing community, society, and world, based in love. We change the world as we change ourselves.

Extend Compassion and Prayer to the Entire Web of Life

We are faced with critical environmental issues today that threaten not only to leave future generations with depleted and polluted resources, but also to undermine our ability to improve the quality of life for Third World peoples. Exercise your projection of energy in this setting as you would with situations involving individuals. Look at situations related to logging of ancient forests, pollution of water resources, endangerment of animals, or overdevelopment of natural habitats. Become the people involved. Become the earth, the animals, and the plants. Feel the pain of being torn apart. Become the machinery of destruction; become the developers and the polluters. Act without judgment and send the energy of love through prayer to all persons, living creatures, and objects associated with the problems of the environment. Let the positive energy contribute to the divine solution for all concerned. The spirits within all that inhabits the earth—both living and that which appears inanimate—are the recipients of your love and positive energy. Our collective interdependence creates a mutual benefit to all. We are all a part of the web of life and judging others negatively ultimately affects each of us.

The next chapter provides a broader definition of prayer, detailing its benefits and how to maximize its effectiveness.

[1-12] Trudy Bragg. Hypnosis Teacher

Prayer

Prayer is focused energy directed to God. Developing a healthy prayer life is part of the dedication that is required for the journey on the spiritual path. Prayer can take many forms—formal, informal, casual, elegant, spoken, silent. All are acceptable, and all are heard. There is no right way to pray, however, some prayers can be extremely powerful. If it comes from the heart, and you understand the laws of energy, prayer can be truly miraculous.

Prayer is a powerful energy. It not only connects you to the Force greater than self, but it stimulates the power of creative energy within you and puts into action your ability to create. You literally merge energies with Creator. You step beyond limitations and into the realm of possibilities. It is a powerful means of adding energy to one's desires. Each time you pray, you add layers of energy to your desires. Thought forms emerge and energy multiplies. The more faith and trust you have, the faster thought manifests into physical reality.

Prayer is an expression of gratitude, love, and relationship. It helps you center yourself and gives nourishment to the soul. It recognizes your divine connection, reconnects you with your own holiness, and nurtures your relationship with Spirit. Your soul is held in the body—a fragile and limiting vessel. Prayer literally takes you out of your body and the linear mind controlling it, into the nonlinear space of Spirit. It allows you to open up and to *expect* that things can be created that do not yet exist, even things beyond your current grasp. Your soul knows this. Prayer serves as a passageway out of the concrete mind and into the realm of possibilities.

Prayer also serves as a medium for building trust and faith. It is a communication between the universe and yourself that recognizes the divinity in both. It helps you prioritize, reevaluate, self-reflect, and discern your needs and desires. The act of prayer is an expression of your confidence in a larger divine order and in the significance of your own existence. It expresses a faith in life and life's experiences. As you walk the spiritual path, you develop a respect for a Force greater than self. You learn to love life in all of its forms and to treat life with respect and reverence. Prayer becomes an overt way to express this growing awareness to yourself and to the universe.

The longing of the soul for connection is answered in prayer. It is the foundation for spiritual connection. If you desire connection, prayer must be built into your life in a way that will withstand the daily pressures and interruptions of life. The quantity of time is not important, but the priority is.

How to Maximize Your Experience of Prayer

1. *Commit yourself to a daily communication with Spirit through prayer.* Your relationship will be enhanced immeasurably.

2. *Set realistic goals for yourself.* Do not try to set up a monk-like routine if you have not previously incorporated prayer into your life. According to the teachings of hypnosis, it takes twenty-one days to create a new habit. Can you pray ten minutes a day for twenty-one days? If so, you can establish the habit of prayer.

3. *Find a quiet time for prayer.* It may mean you have to get up earlier or stay up later to find a time that will work for you. Once you have established the time, stick to it. Do not let other "busyness" get in the way of your special time.

4. *Give thanks for all things, even for those things that have not yet been manifested.* You will discover that prayers are often answered before they are even asked.

5. *Remember that prayer is energy and follows universal laws.*

    Negative energy begets negative energy. Always state desires positively. If you say to Spirit, "I want a new job. I hate this one, it is terrible," the resultant energy is about wanting, hating, and sadness or anger. Energy does not evaluate; it merely multiplies and manifests. Eventually, the negativity of your energy will make the job more and more difficult. Alter the energy by reframing the prayer to say, "Thank you, Great Spirit, for the divine job. Thank you for open doors of new opportunities."

    Requests for the future stay in the future. Claim your desires in the now. Time does not really exist in the spiritual realm. If you are always asking for a wish to be fulfilled someday in the future, then your wish will continue to reside in the future. Your prayer should say, "Thank you for the divine job now." *Now* carries much power.

    Doubts negate prayers. If you are praying with a positive attitude but are thinking, "This is ridiculous. I don't have my divine job and never will," your energy of doubt and fear will counteract the positive energy you generated in your prayer. If you pray for ten minutes, giving it all your heart, and then spend the rest of the day thinking about how undeserving you are, how things never really work out for you, and doubting that your prayer could ever be answered, which outcome receives the most energy? A ten-minute prayer cannot compensate for a day of negative thoughts.

The faith and beliefs behind your prayers will manifest. What you manifest will be in direct proportion to the amount of faith you possess. Jesus, Buddha, the holy ones, healed by faith. They never questioned their power of manifestation. Their faith was/is pure. No doubts filled their minds. Their hearts were filled with love, gratitude, and thankfulness.

6. *Faith and your level of trust will determine your relationship with Spirit.* Prayer requires faith, a belief in the unseen, that which cannot be proven. It is "knowing" with an assurance that defies the rational mind. Faith with trust can only be established through having an intimate relationship with Spirit. All relationships are as strong as the trust embodied in them, and a relationship with God is no different.

7. *Establish a ritual space for your prayer.* Creating a sacred space for prayer supports your prayer and enhances your state of awareness. It brings honor and reverence to the process of praying and declares that you are taking the time and energy to connect with Spirit. You create this sacred space through intention. Although there is no defined protocol for the appearance of sacred space, some of these hints might help you create a space of your own:

   The space is personal and will reflect you and what you believe. It can be a single Buddhist pillow in an empty room or a fancy decorated altar. Keep it holy by respecting it.

   Choose objects that have meaning to you. Choose wisely and remember your objects will carry energy. The energy is real and it will have an impact on the energy of your prayers. Take care of your sacred items—clean them and honor them for it is through them that you are connecting.

   Ask the place if it would like to honor you and your prayers. In the process of choosing your place, always ask. Asking is a major component of respect for all things, including places. The answer will become clear to you.

Dedicate the space with a ritual of some sort. You might sing, pray, chant, rattle, drum, meditate, or bless the space with water. Use your imagination. Whatever works to make the place feel special and cleansed will be appropriate. Be still and notice what you feel, hear, and see, and what your intuition is saying to do. Draw energy down from above and up from the earth; fill your spot with divine light.

After the ordination of your sacred space, it will become your holy place of prayer. With love, respect, and honoring of the space, it literally becomes sacred. When you enter, it will be for prayer and meditation, a time when you and Creator share in building your relationship.

My Own Sacred Space

When people walk into my office where I do my prayers, most say, "It feels wonderful in here." They are responding to my intention, to the love, energy, and relationship I have built with Spirit in my room. My space reflects my extremely eclectic belief system. I have everything from angels to animal bones in my sacred space. I also like to honor Spirit with fresh flowers on my altar—usually roses—as a gift from my heart. My particular spirit allies love roses and I can feel the energy of delight when I place them on my altar. When the roses die, I gather the petals and sprinkle them under my favorite Douglas Fir tree as a gift to the forest, always thankful and grateful for what Spirit brings to my life. My intent is to be conscious of my interconnection with all things. Everything is done from genuine love and respect. I believe that all acts of respect help to build my relationship with Spirit and enhance the energy of my prayers.

As you sit at the same place each day to pray, you will find that your space will begin to accumulate a tremendous amount of energy. This energy stays and lingers in your sacred place. The thought form created by your daily prayers will reinforce stilling the mind, settling into prayer, and connecting with Spirit. You energetically react, so your entire being prepares for prayer as soon as you enter this space. Each day this thought form builds energy and multiplies. It quickens your state of awareness and opens your nonlinear mind. With time you will discover that the moment you enter your sacred space, you fill with the sacred energy of prayer and meditation.

You have probably noticed thought forms of sacred energy in places you have visited. Have you ever walked into a sacred temple, a church, a beautiful setting in nature, a Sundance arbor, or other holy setting where you could feel the power of the place? Innately you knew that something sacred or holy took place in this space. This energy affected you in some way. This is because the energy of prayer or holy intention lingers in such sacred spots. I remember a hike I took in Hawaii. At a certain location I suddenly became keenly aware of sacred energy all around me. I could feel the presence of love, sexuality, and intimacy. Upon inquiring about the area, I learned it was the site of holy ceremony—usually weddings—that the natives of the island still performed there.

Pray mindfully and with an open heart. Respect all things. Be thankful. Create a sacred space with honor, intention, and love. In these ways you will add energy to the universe that will change your life and the lives of countless others.

Questions to Ponder

What does your prayer life look like? What kind of relationship do you have with Source? Are you satisfied with your relationship with Spirit? With the universe? How much effort do you put into this relationship? In comparison to other relationships you have, how much time does God get?

Prayer establishes this relationship. If you are unhappy with your prayer life, then the next question would be, how can you change it? What do you want it to look like? You need to decide how it will work in your life. How much time and effort are you willing to invest in prayer? Do you want a relationship with Spirit or do you want to just request from Spirit? You always have these choices.

If prayers can be sent to Spirit by thoughts, then thoughts are prayers. If thoughts are prayers, then what have you been praying all day?

Faith and Miracles

People who have power—spiritual power—are people who have learned how to work with energy. Working with energy requires an understanding of both scientific laws and universal laws. Scientific laws change as science progresses. There were once laws that supported the beliefs that the earth was flat, was the center of the universe, and that light only travels in a straight line. These laws held true until science advanced to discover other possibilities, at which time new scientific laws emerged. In other words, scientific "proof" supports a set of beliefs until a new scientific model redefines reality. Many scientific truths have passed into myth. Bear in mind that "myth" only exists from the vantage of hindsight; it was "truth" in the context of the time that spawned it.

If history is an accurate predictor of our future, then we must assume that the current scientific "truths" will eventually become myth as new "truths" emerge. How confident of our scientific truths can or should we be? The American dramatist Arthur Miller observed, "An era can be said to be at an end when its basic illusions are exhausted." Our mental models of reality may never be more than "illusions" that we, as a culture, have commonly agreed upon. The models have the feel of truth because they are widely shared. They create our current paradigm.

A paradigm is a constellation of concepts, values, perceptions, and practices shared by a community. That constellation forms the basis for how a community defines and organizes itself. Scientific paradigms, widely accepted by "advanced" societies, have become the basis of defining reality for our world community. "Primitive" societies that may not share our scientific worldviews are often targets of programs intended to "convert" them to our "higher" truths. At times, however, we have discovered that the primitive paradigms were, in fact, accurate. A good example is recent medical discoveries that validate the potency of traditional medicines and the role of mind-body-spirit connection in the healing process. Once considered to be of the realm of "witch doctors," these are now receiving serious attention from the scientific community.

Our beliefs—even our scientific knowledge—color our observations and perceptions. We look for evidence to corroborate what we know; we find the evidence because that is what we are predisposed to see. Consequently, we continually reinforce as true that which we already know. This is done at a subconscious level, but it is how the paradigms govern our lives. Breaking out of these paradigms is difficult, and it takes strong character to go against such compelling and accepted societal norms. History is full of accounts of people being persecuted and, in some instances, killed because they supported new discoveries in science. Hindsight being 20/20, two hundred years later it is easy to say, "How could they have believed something so ridiculous?" What will be said of our beliefs two centuries from now?

In truth, all things are possible and people are limited only by their own imaginations! That is exactly why the spirits are forever asking us to broaden our perspectives.

Our belief systems affect our manifestations, including healings or what are commonly referred to as miracles. According to the information from my spirit teachers, there is no hierarchy of miracles. It is no more difficult to heal cancer than it is to soothe a stubbed toe. The possibility of healing, or the lack thereof, lies in the belief system of the wounded or the healer/practitioner. Healings and miracles deal with energy and the amount of faith or trust contributing to the process.

Faith is built by the strength of one's belief systems. The more you believe something to be true, the more faith you have in the processes associated with it. The more faith you have in the process, the more energy the process will receive. The more energy received, the more fuel to create the desired outcome. As you manifest more and more in your life, your trust level will escalate. As your trust escalates, it feeds energy to your faith and your belief system and thus increases your ability to heal or to perform miracles. This diagram illustrates this cyclical process.

The Process of Faith Building:
Creating Healing and Miracles

Each positive outcome reinforces faith and trust,
creating greater energy toward future positive outcomes.

According to universal law, you will be adding energy either to your faith or to your doubts. The cycle in the illustration is just as true for negative beliefs. When doubt creeps into your awareness, you lose power. If you add energy to your doubts, they will manifest. You reinforce whatever belief system gets the most energy.

It is also important to remember that hope is not the same as faith. Hope is an indicator of lack of faith. Complete faith is absolute; there are no doubts, no fears, no wishing, and no hoping. If you hope for something to happen, you cancel some of its probability.

Until you know absolute faith, some of the upper level energy movement practices will be unattainable by you. You will still, somewhere in your belief system, create a hierarchy of difficulty in which you believe some things are beyond your abilities. This is why many of the so-called miracles are not accessible to many people; they do not have the faith to support moving energy in that way. Doubt extinguishes possibility.

Some examples of activities attainable by working with energy are: shape-shifting, walking on water, fire-walking, and levitating. All are possible. Many of you, as you consider the nature of these activities; have just assigned a level of difficulty to each of these feats. This hierarchy of difficulty is established based on your belief system. If you have heard of something happening, then it brings it into the realm of possibility. These feats actually occur in physical reality. *Shape-shifting*, for example, is not just an awareness one might have in an altered state of consciousness, but actual transformation into another physical form that is able to maneuver in the physical world we commonly share.

If you know the story of Jesus *walking on water*, but have heard of no other person performing the feat, then walking on water might remain, in your thinking, a case of "He can, I cannot." Your need for cumulative evidence will limit your beliefs about your own abilities.

Levitation is the ability to defy gravity. Mystics have been known to do this for centuries. Yogis do it regularly during meditation. Saint Theresa of Avila was said to levitate every time she prayed; she would actually float to the ceiling. Her love for God was greater than any gravitational pull, and she floated upward because of her heart's desire to merge with her beloved Jesus. There are many historical accounts of levitation, but still levitation remains one of the more difficult beliefs to accept.

Fire-walking also defies physical law as we understand it. Fire burns when brought into contact with human flesh. Yet fire-walking has been done for centuries, and many people have heard of it. The mere fact of hearing about a feat brings it into the realm of possibility. Since more people have heard of acts of fire-walking than of levitation, for example, fire-walking actually has the greater potential for being possible. More people are "fueling the thought form" of fire-walking as a possible reality; hence, fire-walking is becoming accessible to more people.

People walk across red-hot coals and glowing rocks that range in temperature from 1000 to 1500 degrees Fahrenheit and do not get burned. Their feet do not even get warm. I have fire-walked myself a total of eleven times. The first time I walked on fire, the group I was participating with was actually filmed for a news broadcast. During the broadcast, aired a month after our fire-walk, the newsperson not only had clips of us fire-walking, she also decided to get different opinions on how this was possible. She interviewed a fire marshal whose attempted explanation of the phenomenon was almost comical. Explanations I have personally heard range from the sweat on one's feet creating a water barrier, to the ash acting like an insulator, to the suggestion that people must soak their feet in ice water before they go across. The plain fact is—you just do not burn. To me, fire-walking felt like walking over popcorn; it crunched, and sometimes poked, but it did not burn. The red embers look like the perfect campfire for roasting marsh-mallows—the hottest form of campfire, more so than when it is flaming. So how can this be? Fourteen hundred degrees is red, scorching, searing, blistering, and glowing hot—a temperature that should cause permanent damage, according to our physical laws of science.

I remember when I was a young girl of about twelve, watching a movie on television. I do not remember the title of the film but it left an impression on me. It took place on a South Sea island. A white sailor had come to visit the island and fell in love with the tribal chief's beautiful daughter. This created quite a stir with the natives, and it was decided that if his love were true, he would be able to walk across fire rocks. The woman was against his proving his love in this way; she believed his love was true, and she did not want him to take the chance of becoming permanently crippled from severe burns. In the movie, there was another island across the bay where many people struggled to survive after being crippled from walking on fire rocks. The central question in the movie was: How pure was the hero's love and how clear was his intention? On the day of the challenge, the heroine stood at the end of the fire rocks awaiting her lover. The intensity of the heat caused perspiration to bead up on not only the hero but on all the people watching. He carefully placed each foot squarely on the searing rocks and slowly walked across. His eyes never came unlocked from the face of his beloved. He never flinched; his body never responded in pain. His feet did not burn. Each step was slow and filled with intention—the intention of proving his love, his devotion, and his integrity. With his last step, he embraced his love. The whole village was now convinced of his undying love.

Even at the age of twelve, this type of pure intent imprinted on my soul. I have been intrigued with fire-walking ever since. I have often wondered how I could ever be that clear, that lacking in doubt, that loving. I wanted to try. I wanted to fire-walk. The opportunity presented itself several years later, all with divine timing.

My scenario was quite a bit different from a South Sea island, but the fact remained that the fire was 1400 degrees, red hot, glowing, and intense. I stood at the beginning of the fire bed staring at the other side, which was about fifteen feet away. I was in a group of about ten people and we had been chanting a song:

> "Earth, my body,
> Water, my blood,

Air, my breath,
And fire, my spirit."

Its tune rhythmically repeated over and over in my mind. The excitement and energy swirled around the others and me. I felt connected to nature, to the fire, and to my spirit allies. My bare feet were tingling from the immense amount of energy running through my body. I felt a force vibrating in my muscles and deep within my being.

I had participated in the building of the fire, embellishing each log with my prayers. I ignited the kerosene soaked logs and watched a blaze leap and dance fifteen feet into the air. We waited two hours for the heat to intensify, burning the wood to its hottest point. I participated in raking the burning embers into the sculptured runway that we would walk across. My hands burned from the intense heat rising up from the sizzling wood and the rake handle grew hot to the touch. My face was flushed and hot, sweltering from the heat. The whole process brought me intimately close to the intensity of the heat, to the fire, and to the reality of my quest. I had become invested in the fire and felt a kinship with it.

As I stood there ready to walk, I called to my spirit allies and felt them swirling around me. I set my intention; it was simple and precise, "I am walking to the other side."

I stood at the threshold of a moment of truth. The heat of the embers and the smell of the smoke intruded momentarily into my senses, but they seemed overwhelmed by the faith that had built within me. I found all the scientific laws I had learned being replaced by the natural laws of the universe I had come to know. What was to prove true in this moment was not a part of the "truths" I had been taught by the world, but those I had been taught by Spirit.

When I raised my foot from the coolness of the dirt edging the pit, I did so without hesitation or trepidation. I had anticipated a test of wills between the fire and myself. I had expected to draw on my inner and physical strength to resist the intensity of the heat. It was to prove otherwise.

I stepped out onto the burning wood and started across. I was immediately surprised that I felt no heat on my feet; not just an absence of burning, but actually an absence of any heat at all. The only physical sensation was a hard, crunchy feeling as I placed each foot one before the other as I moved across the burning wood. I was not competing or resisting the fire—our strong spirits honored and respected each other. There was no contest of wills, only a merging of the fire's powerful spirit with my own.

A fire capable of consuming flesh did not deny me. It invited and understood the changes in my soul—the vanishing of learned fears and the growth of courage and confidence. What the spirits had been teaching me about faith, about transcending physical law, about willingness, had just become a physical reality. Concepts became real and tangible and set into my cells as experience: Unexplainable perhaps to the mental mind, but real just the same. The walk was exhilarating, an empowering journey without fear or pain. I made it to the other side.

My faith soared in the process. I was elated and high on life from what I had just done. I had to do it again. That night I went over the fire several times. With each experience, I built tremendous trust in the process. At the end of the night I was completely empowered.

I thought, "Just look at what I have done!"

I felt that anything was now within my grasp.

These feelings held true for everyone in my group. A buzz of conversation ensued. Everyone laughed easily and shared the excitement and sense of accomplishment. There was giddiness to the occasion—all earlier efforts at focus and preparation were now replaced by giggles and laughter. The energy remained high, but there was an almost audible release of tension. It was like moving from holding one's breath to squeals of delight. The initial sense of apprehension was replaced by elation at having mastered one's fear. All were ecstatic.

Fire-walking is about love, intention, willingness, and mystery. The outcomes of this experience were happiness, trust, faith, and empowerment. Not a bad set of results! Fire-walking is just one way the spirits have physically taught me that all things are possible. I learned firsthand that fire-walking cannot be explained by the rational mind, and to attempt to do so is a waste of energy. I also learned that intention and belief alter physical law, even the law that says, "Fire burns, fire kills, fire disfigures."

The spirits again brought home the fact that we, as humans, are only limited by our own minds, our belief systems, and our fears.

Since this experience, Spirit has taught me much about manmade laws and physical laws. We need them to help us understand our world and to explain why things work the way they do. They provide a tremendous amount of safety to our frail humanness. However, when working with Spirit, we are capable of altering any of our frailties. Spirit is not limited by gravity, fire, the speed of light, time, or locality. All is possible. Belief in such feats is non-rational, requiring that one be able to move beyond rational thought to understand that the universal consciousness dwarfs our rational minds.

The Native Americans have a term that is used for Spirit, for All. They refer to the Great Mystery. It is a perfect expression. Spirit is a mystery and should stay that way. Some things are not to be explained. When we explain, we limit. When we believe in the Great Mystery, we see the possible in the impossible and understand that which cannot be explained. The rational mind limits possibilities, growth, discoveries—it limits you.

Spirit wants us to change from the question, "How can that be done?" to the statement, "I can do that."

There are volumes written about faith, but the concept is as simple as the mystery it defines. Faith is the belief in the unseen, not the seen. Spirit is asking us to have faith and trust Spirit, trust the mystery, trust the unexplainable. Trust is developed from experience, even if our experience includes not being able to explain why something happened. When faith and trust are developed, we open ourselves up to the unexplainable truth of Spirit. It is mind boggling, many times incomprehensible, and it is supposed to be so. It is the Great Mystery.

How much do you trust Spirit? Are you willing to let go and surrender to the process of change that is essential for spiritual growth? Lao Tzu in the *Tao Te Ching* wrote, "True mastery can be gained by letting things go their own way. It cannot be gained by interfering." You cannot and should not control the world about you, but you must surely participate actively. Mastery is being in the natural flow of the universe and allowing yourself to move to a new place.

Imagine this scenario. You are asking or praying for some sort of physical healing. You are motivated and enthused, dedicating time to meditation and prayer, running energy through your body, and doing all the things you believe are good for you. Suddenly you lose your job. You are shocked, disillusioned, and fearful. You feel insecure, and lose your focus on your healing and your faith in Spirit. You have difficulty accepting an event that does not fit with your sense of what healing should look like. Consider the possibility that your job is the cause of an energy creating your illness. Consider that you might need to live in some other part of the country and that your job has been an impediment to that move. Consider that the nature of your work has made you unhappy; creating negative energy that contributes to your need for healing. *Trust the things that happen.* What appears negative to you may, in fact, be necessary for your spiritual awakening. Be thankful. And try to develop a larger awareness of how things unfold for growth and healing. Look positively ahead and contribute positive energy to whatever will be your next experience. Maintain your commitment. Trust that the events will take you to a good place.

Your prayers are answered, you are loved, and there is a divine order to life. *Miracles happen!*

Rituals and Ceremonies

The nature of ritual is that it supports change. Rituals are performed to make something happen, invoke spiritual power, or identify something as sacred. They are designed to transcend the linear mind, stimulate the senses, and open the subconscious to inner work, inner change, and transformation. I think of ceremonies as celebrations and often use the words interchangeably. Both rituals and ceremonies can help you experience Spirit in a profound and dynamic way. They help to declare your intentions and to acknowledge the spirits as magnificent beings.

No matter what your background, you have been exposed to ritual and ceremony. Cultures create different traditions to honor the spirit realm, but there are many commonalities throughout the world. All cultures and societies have rituals such as funerals, weddings, celebrations of birth, and other transitions in life. Rituals are often used as rites of passage to mark stages of change in one's lifetime. Many indigenous cultures have a rite of passage for young men. In Native American tribes, young men commonly participated in a twenty-four hour vision quest where they were placed on a hill by their mothers and brought back from their experiences by their fathers. The quest marked their transition to manhood.

Benedictions, sacraments, candlelight services, chorus singing, prayer, invoking the directions, blessing-way ceremonies, sweat lodges, vision quests, sun dances, darmas, and chanting are all forms of calling Spirit to join in a special way to bless and to guide. Rituals promote a giving and sharing of information between you and Spirit, each of you benefiting the other. I have found, repeatedly and without exception, that if you ask with an attitude of respect for help from the spirit realm, it will be available to you. Rituals and ceremonies do just that. They serve as the invitation to Spirit that says, "Join me. Bless this time. I honor your presence and your existence. I believe in you; help me connect to you in a powerful way. Let me feel you around me and inside of me. Merge with me."

Rituals and ceremonies can be done privately or publicly. Just bowing your head before a meal and thanking Spirit for the bounty of your table is a ceremony. The more you do ritual and ceremony *with intention* and love, the more you will come to know the marvelous energy of the spirit realm. After all, if you want to walk the spiritual path, then you need to acknowledge Spirit and start defining and developing your relationship.

The Spirit Realm

The recognition of your connection will alter your consciousness; you will become more awake and more aware. The spirit realm is infinite and holistic. It includes the ethereal energies—angels, animal spirits, nature spirits, saints, the master teachers such as Jesus and Buddha, ancestors, gods, and goddesses. The spirits also exist in nature, in the trees, in the plants, in the air—in all the elements of our natural environment. There is life beyond what the human eye sees. If you use the eyes of your heart, you can sense it. Rituals and ceremonies assist you with this awareness and honor the spirit lives.

All things have a spirit, and the practices of ceremony and ritual require that one recognize this. The rocks, trees, land, birds, animals, fish, air, water, thunder, the earth, minerals, crystals, plants, flowers, stars, moon, and planets—all have a spirit and a divine purpose. We are in relationship to all of this life. The Lakota term *mitakuye oyasin* means "we are all related." The awareness of interconnectedness and relationship is ancient. Our forefathers understood because they lived close to nature. They recognized the interrelationship with nature's forces and did not seek dominion over them. Today, few people come out of their homes or their work places to connect to life and the spirits of nature. In modern culture, mankind has tried to dominate nature, denying the mutual benefit. Our ego, our attitudes, and our intellect so often cause us confusion about our connection with life and God. Being awake, or conscious, means tuning into this interconnectedness again. You must develop a relationship with the nature spirits as well as your helping spirits of the ethereal realm.

The directions east, south, west, north, above, below, and within have spiritual natures and are often invoked in sacred ceremonies. The medicine wheel teachings refer to these directions and their spiritual natures using archetypes. These archetypes explain the core of being and the cycles of life. The medicine wheel teachings are ancient and cross-cultural. The teachings can have a profound effect on you, heightening awareness when interwoven into your daily life.

Things that are not human, such as the spirits of nature, have a purity of spirit. They lack ego. Things of nature are what they are; they have purpose, they have spirit, and they have been placed on the planet for divine reason. Their connection and purpose are never confused. Indigenous cultures understood that rocks hold great wisdom. An individual rock may have been around for thousands or millions of years. The spirit contained in the rock holds memory of creation and ancient knowledge that it will generously share with you as you build a relationship with it. It magically transforms into the wise elder, with whom you can communicate telepathically from the heart.

The same interaction connects you to the plant nation. Plants hold the wisdom for healing, the cures for disease, and the wisdom of nutrition. Place a plant leaf in your hand or lean up against a tree; still yourself and your mind. Center down into your heart and ask. These spirits are here to serve you, to be in relationship with you, to help you heal and be well. They will advise and teach if you just learn to ask. They also bring you happiness, divine beauty, and joy. Respect them, honor them, take care of them, and ask them questions. Learn from them the knowledge they hold.

One day I was in the forest behind my house digging up ferns I wanted to transplant to my yard. The way that I normally approach such an activity is to walk along asking (silently or aloud, depending on who's around) which plants would like to be in my yard and asking their permission to dig them up. I also sprinkle tobacco as a gift or offering to them. Tobacco offerings are a Native American tradition I love. However, on this particular day, there was a storm threatening. I was tired and began to hurry. After I had transplanted four or five ferns, I forgot my tobacco offerings and my asking. I began digging the ferns that were close and easy, with no communication.

I was bent over, pulling and straining, trying to dislodge a particular plant, when I got smacked on my behind so hard it knocked me off balance. I had to step forward to prevent myself from falling. It created quite the sting on my bottom. As I was attempting to steady myself, I turned around expecting to see my husband. I figured he had walked up behind me and gotten too aggressive with his greeting. As I was about to blurt out my complaint, I realized that there was no human present. I stood there shocked, trying to figure out who had hit me. I even rationalized that I had stepped on my shovel and the handle had sprung up, but the shovel was lying several feet away. As I stood there baffled, an awareness flowed through me. I heard Spirit speak loud and clear through the multi-levels of my mind, "Do not get so hasty, dear one. Ask before you take, and always say thank you."

I stared at the fern, questioning the reality of this strange occurrence. My bottom was still stinging. I tried to still myself, tuning in to the messages. I had been reminded that my relationship with the spirits was real and must be taken seriously.

The teachings of this experience are multi-layered, as are most teachings. The most obvious lesson was, once you know protocol, it becomes expected behavior.

I knew better than to take without asking and to show reverence and respect for my sisters and brothers of the forest. I was accountable for my relationship with the spirits of nature and for the respect shared between us. This accountability is part of the spiritual path, of being awake and aware. This was by no means a punishment or retribution; it was just Spirit's way of reminding me of my responsibility.

Every time the spirits help, guide, or direct you, they are honoring you and your earth-walk. In return, you must respect and honor the spirits. Honoring is a sacred teaching, and is part of the work of anyone seeking heightened consciousness.

When the spirits reach out to you in a tangible way, pay attention. I have heard so many stories where people, trying to rationally explain them, dilute such experiences. Do not do that to yourself. Find the teaching instead.

When you become awake and aware of the presence of Spirit, a whole new reality presents itself, and it can be life changing. You will cultivate a great respect for life. As you develop rituals and ceremonies, honor these spirits of life. Invite them into your life, your sacred space, your ceremony. Welcome them and thank them. They offer abundance. They heal, they teach, and they are the bringers of understanding and wisdom. Honor them.

The spirits do respond to ritual and ceremony. This is a guarantee. They will read your heart, your integrity, and respond by either showing up or not. As you become more familiar with being conscious of what you are doing and why you are doing it, you will actually begin to feel the spirits enter when you begin a ceremony or ritual. Sometimes it will be an awareness of their presence, a knowing, or a sensing; other times it may be an actual physical touch, sound, or smell, but you will know. I have developed a relationship with the spirits that is like a fascinating magical friendship. I say hello to them, I bring them gifts, and I interact with them consistently. They also show their reverence to me in a regular and respectful way. They often touch me, and, at times, I see them or hear them. I am always aware of them. The tangible signs come in various ways for different people and often at the least expected times. It is nothing that you can force. When they show themselves physically, it is a gift from them to honor the relationship you have cultivated.

The Sweat Lodge Ceremony

I have had many wonderful opportunities in my life. One of these has been to participate regularly in the Native American Inipi Ceremony; more commonly called the sweat lodge. The sweat lodge is a customary ceremony and is used regularly for purification, prayer, and healing. It is like church for the Native American. I revere this ceremony, for it has repeatedly brought me divine connection and awareness.

Everything about the sweat lodge is sacred. It is built with intention and prayer. Each item used in the ceremony serves a divine purpose. The sweat lodge represents the womb of Mother Earth, who gave life to us all. The sweat lodge is often constructed with red willow branches, which are tied together in a frame representing the ribs of Mother Earth. The dome shape of the lodge is much like that of a pregnant woman's belly. This dome is covered with blankets and quilts, leaving space for the door. When the door is closed, there is no light on the inside. This darkness is like the inside of the womb of the sacred mother.

A hole is dug in the center of the sweat lodge floor, the earth from which is used to make an altar in front of the door. The hole or pit will receive the hot stones (the stone people) when they are brought from the fire into the sweat lodge. The altar is used for sacred and special items to be blessed.

Once everyone is seated inside the sweat lodge, the heated stone people are brought in. The person pouring the sweat—the ceremony leader—will determine how many stones come into the lodge at a time. There are four rounds to the sweat, with each round consisting of closing the door, pouring water on the rocks to create an intense steam, and opening the door briefly at the end of each round. The ceremony is actually the sweating out of impurities from the system—creating purification and healing. During the sweat there is much singing, drumming, invoking the spirits, and praying. The sacred songs generate a great deal of power in the ceremony.

Each detail of the ceremony holds meaning. It is very involved and extremely sacred. Out of respect for the ancient teachings, and the elders who taught me, I will not divulge the details of the ceremony in the way I have learned it. I have explained as much as I have to capture a visual image of the event. My story actually begins here.

On one occasion, I was participating as a supporter during a vision quest ceremony. I was one of many people who stayed in camp during the four-day ceremony. Supporters play an important role in the vision quest because they support the energy of the ceremony through prayer, fostering love, and connection for those on the quest.

Around midnight on one day of the vision quest, I was sitting with seven other women in a sweat lodge ceremony. I did not know any of the women well, and only a couple by name. It felt good to be in the sweat lodge, and I was glad there were only a few of us; it made movement in the lodge easier and more comfortable. I still placed myself as close as I could to the pit in the center of the lodge where the red hot, glowing rocks are placed. I love to feel the intense heat and steam, and to smell the sweet grass and lavender as it is brushed on the fiery rocks when they enter the lodge. I settled myself, trying to find a level spot on the ground. I crossed my legs, pulled my back up straight, and began to smile. I love the whole event, and it always makes me feel blessed. I knew this would be a time of feeling close to God, to Spirit. I was happy I could support others through the power and intention of my own prayer. The door closed, darkness enveloped us, and the first round began.

The songs are now familiar and I can sing them with intention, love, and meaning. The variety of voices, the poetic sounds of the indigenous language and the drum make for a mesmerizing experience. As I sang, I could hear the water being poured onto the rocks that hiss as the water meets the heat. The water pourer was sitting across the pit from me at a distance of perhaps five feet. The women on both sides of me were within arm's reach. We formed an irregular circle. The steam and heat were increasing and I began to sweat. It felt good.

I was engrossed in song and sweating profusely when feathers slapped me on the forehead. At first I was pleased. I thought the water pourer was making rounds greeting the circle of women with her eagle feather fan. But soon the slapping became too strong and I reached out, trying to persuade whoever was doing this to move on to the next person. I waved my hands through the air, trying to find a body attached to the feathers. I had never participated in a sweat with this particular water pourer, so I had no idea what particular style she used in conducting the sweat. After several seconds, the hitting stopped. The round ended, the door opened, and the steam dissipated. Since it was midnight, only a minimal amount of light crept in through the door, but it was enough for me to notice that everything appeared quite normal. Whoever had been doing the greeting was seated again.

The second round came and the same situation occurred. The feathers hit me quite roughly on the center of my forehead. I again searched with my hands for some human shape to identify. My body retracted from the slapping of the feathers. I did not want to be rude and turn away, but I was feeling like enough was enough and I pulled back. Then my rational mind kicked in. I realized I was sitting right up against the stones, which meant there was no room for anyone in front of me. The steam was so intense that anyone reaching across the pit would surely have been burned. No one could stay in that position for long. How was she doing this and how was she able to get around in pitch dark? I could not see a thing. I assumed she was just really good at this. I was puzzled and could come up with no other explanation.

During the third round, the scenario changed a bit. Again the door was closed, the darkness invaded our space, and the steam intensified. The songs began. To my amazement, feathers again slapped me, but this time it was by an entire wing—a huge wing. I assumed it was of an eagle. Eagle wings are traditionally used in Native American ceremonies. The people revere these magnificent birds and regard them as sacred. The wing I now felt extended from the top of my head to my foot, striking my shoulder and knee both at once. Its size was startling, for it was larger than my seated body. I had no idea how far above my head it extended. The wing pounded me intensely, and I still could not figure out who was doing it. I was becoming unnerved.

By the fourth round, my curiosity was rampant. I peeked across to the water pourer before the door closed, trying to see a prop of feathers. I wanted to see the huge eagle wing, but it was too dark. The door closed and the next round began. I felt no feathers this time, but instead a rattle came right to my forehead and rattled in front of my brow and around my head. My innocence and curiosity kept me from panicking. The rattle was loud and very close. If I moved, I would surely be struck by it. I sat still, enjoying the sound, amazed that anybody could achieve this in the dark. I was quite impressed, and assumed that all the women were being greeted like this.

When the sweat was over, no one was in a hurry to leave. The atmosphere was relaxed as we sat and talked. I decided to ask about the feathers.

I began with, "Sister, may I ask a question?"

She said, "Yes."

"How did you manage to come around to greet us all with the eagle feathers when we were sitting so close to the pit? Weren't you afraid of falling in?"

She looked startled and replied, "I didn't greet you with feathers. I don't even have my feathers in the lodge."

My mouth dropped open. I continued, "But the feathers were hitting me and the rattle traveled around my head."

She replied, "I have a rattle, but I only used it here by my side."

I was stunned. My eyes searched the faces of the other women. Hadn't they experienced this also? Wasn't the greeting for everyone? Their faces indicated I alone had experienced this phenomenon. Had Spirit approached me so specifically and so adamantly? Could this be true? Could Spirit have appeared so physically, so real? My mind flashed back to the event as it had taken place. I remembered my hands reaching out to touch a body but never finding one.

Never had I considered that it might be Spirit controlling the feathers, or that they were spirit feathers. I felt inadequate, like I had lost touch with reality. I kept replaying the events in my mind. I remembered the feeling in each round, when the feathers approached me, how long they stayed, the difference between the single feather fan and the feather wing, the rattle and its piercing sound. Could what I was thinking be true? I checked my position; I was just inches from the stone pit. It would have been impossible for a human being to maneuver in the space provided. The pourer couldn't have reached across. It was too far, the stones too intensely hot, the steam too burning. And she had just denied doing so.

I was flooded with thoughts of this amazing experience. I started to question my reactions. If I had known that it was Spirit approaching me, would I have acted differently? Would I have tried to look for the message Spirit was providing? Would I have bowed my head in honor? Would I have been scared? I knew I wouldn't have been so irreverent as to urge Spirit to move on to the next person! I had been in lodges before where Spirit was very apparent; this is a reality of the sweat lodge ceremony. And Spirit has often made itself known to me through flashing lights or sound; it always brings me great joy when Spirit can be seen or heard. But this was different. I had been singled out. Why? What was Spirit saying to me? Had I done something wrong? Was I sick? My inner knowing kept saying, "No, no, just be still."

I realized that everyone was staring at me. I was shaken, my head spinning, but I stayed in control and did not ask any more questions. After a few more minutes, we were dismissed. I was told to speak with an elder about the event at the completion of the vision questers' ceremony. I was to "be still" with this for at least one more day.

I am usually a calm and grounded person, but this experience had me mystified. The power of the event was overwhelming. I have never felt the magnitude of Spirit so adamantly present. This was much more intense than any former sweat lodge experience. Because I was a vision quest supporter, it was not proper to focus on my experience, nor was there even anyone to discuss it with. I felt very alone with my questions.

My eventual session with a Lakota elder was tearful. I was overwhelmed with emotion. I kept crying during my session. When he asked if I had had the experience because I needed a healing, I kept answering no. A healing would have been the most logical explanation of why Spirit would come so blatantly, but to my knowledge I was fine. My intuition convinced me that it was not a healing I had received—physical, emotional, mental, or spiritual. It felt more like a blessing, an acknowledgement from Spirit to me. But to claim that Spirit had singled me out at someone else's vision quest, for personal acknowledgement, seemed arrogant. I felt open and vulnerable and knew that I needed to process this event in my own home, at my own altar. My emotional response was profound. I felt both out of balance and honored—and terribly confused. I went home and sat with my experience. I journaled, I prayed, I meditated, I journeyed. It actually took two years before I would understand. Finally, after three other events, each event mystical and unexplainable, each event specifically involving the eagle, I received the information from the spirits explaining these experiences. The eagle was coming to me in ordinary reality, entering my physical reality, to offer me its medicine. Medicine, in this sense, is a gift or talent that can be used by the receiver for healing. It is not uncommon for the spirits to offer their medicine while a person is on a shamanic journey in an altered state of consciousness. What is unusual is for the spirit to enter the person's physical reality and to make its presence known in such a tangible way. Spirit chose to come physically into my world to deliver the gift, rather than to wait for me to enter the spiritual realm. I now use the medicine both for myself and for others in my healing work. I am still learning about it and probably will for years to come. I feel blessed and honored.

Spiritual Reality and the Physical World

The spirit world may be accessed by imagination, but its world is not imaginary. Shamans and persons experienced in journeying know that the spirit realm is every bit as real as the world of our daily lives. A Native American elder once told me that the stories of the Christian Bible were more real for him than they are for many Christian priests. He explained that he connected with the spirit world more directly and with a greater sense of its physical truth than one who might see the spirit world as a distant "other world" to be visited after death. The parting of the Red Sea, the burning bush, and the other miracles of the Bible were more understandable to him because similar events had manifested in his own spiritual practice. Western culture depicts its mystical connections in the form of stories and mythology. We have difficulty understanding that the spirit world is an *other reality*, and that it can become a part of our present *conscious reality* if we have the faith and the commitment to allow it. The eagle visit helped me to understand that the spirit world is real, immediate, and accessible. The beating of the eagle's feathers about my head taught me that our daily reality is no more physically real than our spiritual reality. The eagle's gift came to me in innocence; I did not ask for it, but I honor it. I marvel at how Spirit works and how magically present and available Spirit is.

I want readers to note that at certain times it can take years to obtain information about specific subjects. I journeyed on the meaning of the eagle's visit for two years; the spirits continually reinforced that I had been blessed or honored but did not provide me with a complete understanding. This time was very difficult for me. I was used to obtaining the information I needed from the spirit realm quickly; however, time is relative, and I have learned to honor that. I needed to experience the other events that involved the eagle before I could understand the eagle's intention. As a consequence of waiting, I learned about patience, devotion, willingness, and divine timing in all things.

The Spiritual Path

The spiritual path is a path of transition, movement, and change to a higher vibrational level. To make room for the new, we must abandon the old.[1] As with any transition, there is likely to be a certain amount of sorrow inherent in the process. You may experience a period of difficult struggle and wish to abandon the effort altogether, but you must keep your attention on the commitment to your spiritual growth. If your prayer is for enlightenment, you must employ positive energy and trust the process. Spirit perceives the big picture and is working out the dynamics for all concerned. Although difficult, you will look back on this period of transition as a time of your developing strength. Afterward, you will feel stronger, with a greater understanding of yourself and your potential power.

During this time of personal growth, many alterations may occur in relationships with others. Friendships may change, marriages may break up, and families may come apart. Your development, whether it sustains, strengthens, or ends a relationship, is necessary for you. If you do not achieve your essential growth, you will be limiting the positive energy you bring to your environment. Those persons you love will benefit ultimately by your growth.

Making big changes in your life will have a ripple effect. I was once told that each of us at any given moment has 405 helping spirits surrounding us. They are all taking into account your prayers, and are engaged in conversations about the dynamics of your life. When you have made a commitment to change, they attend. They align with your intention and find the events to provide you the support to pursue your journey. Since spiritual growth is a never-ending journey and not an event, these conversations will continue as long as you live, and beyond. Each adjustment may be difficult to understand, but trust the spirits to help you find the path through the turmoil to eventually find yourself.

Honor and Trust in the Relationship with Spirit

Many people start a new commitment to the spiritual path, or start defining their relationship with Spirit, and then immediately want wonderful things to manifest for them. Unfortunately, this is usually unrealistic. Before you are given access to the unlimited information, or powers of the universe, there is a respect and a trust that needs to develop between you and the spirit realm. Just as you are developing trust for the spirits, they are developing a trust for you. You are building a relationship that takes time, effort, and commitment. Once this trust is developed, there is a mutual responsibility and accountability. You can depend on the spirits and they will depend on you.

Spirit will open doors for you at your own individual level. It is like the employee being considered for promotion. As you prove yourself through time and effort, new opportunities will be presented for you to explore how Spirit, life, the laws of nature, and the laws of the universe work. Like a promotion at work, a promotion to greater consciousness comes with greater responsibility.

Knock, and the door will be opened for you; ask, and you shall receive. How true these words are. However, a relationship with Spirit is like building a relationship with a friend. It requires trust, shared experience, dedication, and much interaction. There is much to learn, and one needs to be prepared for the incredible power that becomes available in the learning.

As energy flows with intention between you and Spirit, and between different realities, your personality will change. You are opening your psychic centers and becoming more awake. Your entire being must make adjustments to include your new awareness. Spirit will monitor what you experience and at what levels you are able to receive information. Not only is trust being built between you and Spirit in this approach, but Spirit knows it is often better not to open too fast to new realities because sudden changes can feel chaotic and threatening. If you were suddenly opened up to completely new realities, the accompanying stress might be detrimental to your long-term growth. Spirit wants you to enjoy the transition, not be scared. Emotional breakthroughs may result in emotional breakdowns if you move too quickly. Be patient.

There are numerous accounts of people becoming spiritually awakened through near-death experiences or devastating illnesses; however, the awakening does not need to be so dramatic to create greater awareness and personal power. I often think of this analogy with my children. They love to sit in my lap and steer the car the short distance from the mailbox to the driveway. They insist that I keep my hands off the steering wheel because they want to drive the car by themselves. I reluctantly agree, but my caution comes from knowing they are unaware of the power of this machine. Gradually, they will assume more responsibility for controlling the car, and one day they will be ready to drive solo. Hopefully, their experience will be a positive one. One must enter the spiritual realm in the same way—with care and the expectation of adjustment. Awareness emerges in manageable doses until we are safely prepared. Sudden revelation and epiphany have their place in awakening, but one must not assume that they are the only avenues to enlightenment.

The patient path is one of developing a relationship with Spirit that is filled with integrity, love, and service. Do your part. Pray, meditate, practice journeying, and make yourself available for Spirit to work with you. Show respect for life and live from the heart chakra. Continue to self-examine and be committed to growth and spiritual development. As a demonstration of your effort, log your experiences in a journal. As you read and reread the entries, you will discover a subtle but sure change in your being. Many changes will occur, often without your conscious awareness. The journal will help you to retrace your journey and to recognize these changes. I think you will be amazed at how fast Spirit truly does intervene in your life. Be thankful.

There are many ways to connect with Spirit and finding a way to develop this intimate, personal relationship is up to you.

[1] Eakins, Pamela. *Tarot of the Spirit.* Samuel Weiser, Inc., 1992.

Negative Energy

I bring up the subject of negative energy cautiously because there are many conflicting opinions of not only what it is, but also how it is generated and how it affects us. I believe negative energy is one of the most significant influences in life. It is based in fear and it is, in many respects, the opposite of love. We are all subjected to the negative energies of anger, hatred, and sadness. Many people fear evil forces or have superstitions about dark forces. We are often reluctant to confront the negative forces that course through us because they reveal a dark side of ourselves, which makes us uncomfortable. We became hesitant to continue the self-examination we need. Negative energy creates a huge thought form with a tangible reality and often seems to take on a life of its own. However, understanding negative energy is the first step to conquering the fear that feeds it. Since negative energy is the opposite of love, it is through love that it is conquered.

I have encountered negative energy often in my work. I have been warned, by people who understand the work, that what I do might place me in danger from ominous forces. While doing healing work and soul retrievals, I have found myself in some pretty precarious situations, but the spirits have faithfully protected me and have used these situations to teach me. On one such journey, I found myself in a particularly frightening situation. It was unusual for me because I am conditioned to taking risks and have much confidence in the protection I receive from my spirit allies. Yet in this instance, I was endangered.

A client sought a soul retrieval from me because his life seemed dominated by continuous failures. He had an extremely pessimistic attitude and believed his condition was deteriorating. He hoped to find the lost soul part that denied him the ability to take hold of his life and make positive movement toward healing. I entered the journey and immediately found myself encased in a plexiglass tomb. All motion ceased in the clear hard casing. I could easily see my surroundings but I was incapable of movement. I also found that I could not move my mouth to call for help. I immediately scanned with my eyes and located my power animal. My training in shamanic work causes me to rely on my power animals in difficult situations. They are magical entities that have supernatural powers. However, in this particular situation, my power animal was also suspended motionless in a plexiglass tomb. His dumbfounded expression indicated that he had no answer for me on what to do in this predicament. My supposedly unlimited protection from my spirit allies seemed suddenly very limited. My teachings were failing me and I was overwhelmed with uncertainty as to what to do. I wondered if I would ever be freed of this situation and what would happen next. I felt powerless to save myself.

In a few moments, a bright light appeared. The intensity of the light was so great that its heat began to melt away the plexiglass tomb. Great globs of melted plastic dropped away from my body. Gradually, movement was possible. In a few more moments my power animal and I were freed and we completed the soul retrieval together.

Upon my return to my client, he informed me that when I started the journey he was overwhelmed with a sensation of fear for my safety. He had a very strong sense of the magnitude of his own fear, resistance, and doubts. The negative energy was so powerful in his own thoughts that he imagined I might be in serious danger from the forces that inhabited his soul. He did not stop me from entering the journey, but his fear was palpable.

I described to him the events that had passed on the journey and the feelings I had. The ominous danger he had feared manifested itself in my journey. His fears had taken form from the power of the negative energy he held within. He feared for my safety but was unable to prevent the energy from seizing me and holding me motionless. What came from outside me was the only force capable of vanquishing a power this great. The bright light was, I realized, the power of love—the opposing force to negative energy. I was able to offer this understanding to the client, but I took away a greater awareness also. Negative forces are prevalent in the universe, but we never need to be victimized by them. The positive energy of love transcends and ultimately frees us. No matter how great the forces we struggle against, there is one power always greater—love.

After my client left, I reflected long on the uniqueness of this experience. I realized that the spirits had used the situation, as with previous experiences, to teach me about love and its power over fear—both the fear generated from my own belief system and the fear generated from someone else's. Whether from within or from without, and regardless of its magnitude, the negative energy and fear we face can be overcome.

An important piece to this awareness is an understanding of our own strength. In this journey I found myself without control. I felt helpless to act on my own behalf, but I was without fear. I had only my conviction that I would always be safe if I believed in the miraculous good of the universe. I did not know how I would be saved in this precarious situation; I just knew that I would be. The metaphors of the plastic encasement and bright light were clear to me. We do not seek love; we allow it to come to us. It is by our faith that it finds us. Our efforts must be directed toward suppressing the fears that debilitate us, and allowing the powers available to free us. I considered the consequences that would have ensued in this journey had I allowed my fears to dominate. I suspect that the results would have been far different. I did learn that the spirits' intervention goes beyond anything I might have learned in my shamanic training and that I must always trust.

When dealing with negative energies on any level, it is important to look inward to determine the ways to deal with the specific nature of the negative energy. Scrutinize your own belief system about negative energy to give you clarity. I suggest writing down specific descriptors of the energy, as you see it, and a brief analysis of what you see as its influence on your thoughts and behaviors.

Prayer has tremendously positive effects upon negative energy and can keep you clear of its influence. Shielding yourself from negative energy is very important, especially if you are working around a lot of it or doing healing work for others. Take the time each day to fill yourself with light, or place protective shields around yourself. These work well and are good practices to develop. You activate the shield through intention. It is as simple as imagining a protective energy field being placed around you. Some people give their shield color, like a translucent blue egg; some people believe in the protective qualities of the violet ray and shield themselves with that color; other people use a science fiction type of force field around them. Whatever works for you, use it. Your thoughts will manifest protection if you direct them to do so.

I find that people, who worry a lot about needing to be protected, need a lot of protection. Again, the whole philosophy of needing to be protected comes from your belief system. If you are adding energy to the fact that you need to be protected, you will need to be protected. If you add energy to the belief that you are always protected, that reality will manifest. You decide, as always.

For me, I have a profound trust in the universe and in Light. I believe Light to be the ultimate power and protector. I do not believe I am ever without this protection, so consequently I am not. The analogy that I like to use is a dark empty room. No matter how dark the darkness is, when you walk in and flip on the lights, *all* the darkness disappears. Darkness has no power or existence in the light.

I was traveling one night through the Columbia River Gorge, one of the most beautiful scenic drives in the world. The gorge is breathtaking. It is lined with steep rock walls, whose natural sculpting have been carved into its rocky cliffs by water and wind erosion. The mighty Columbia River flows through this gorge to the Oregon coast and the Pacific Ocean. The highway runs alongside this sacred river, at water level, traveling east to west. The wind howls through the gorge with ferocity, transforming it into a giant wind tunnel that captures, narrows, and intensifies the wind as it blows from the east. During the winter, because of its steep massive rock sides, traveling up out of the gorge from the highway can be dangerous. Icy conditions and gale force winds make for deadly driving.

It was a winter night when I set out with a friend up the gorge. The trip normally takes about two hours, and I thoroughly enjoy it when the roads are clear. I had listened for the weather report and even made a few calls about road conditions. It appeared that conditions would allow for an uneventful trip, but there was a storm brewing that was to hit late that night or the following morning. I decided to prepare for spending the night just in case I got stranded. If the storm held off, we hoped to be home by midnight.

I was driving a fairly new minivan and felt safe and comfortable. My friend and I chatted excitedly about the trip and what the evening might hold for us. Even though it was only 5:00 p.m., the night was very dark. Darkness sets in early in Northwest winters.

We were well into the trip when the electrical system in my car started going haywire. The outside and the inside lights started to flash on and off, with the control panel and overhead lights creating a strobe light effect in the van. The electric locks suddenly locked and unlocked, up and down, with a startlingly eerie noise. My friend and I gasped at the sudden sound and light show. The car seemed possessed. What paranormal forces were at play here? We stared at each other, not sure whether to laugh at the weirdness of the car's behavior or scream in terror of the unknown.

On this dark night, the car was quite a sight to passing vehicles, as evidenced by the incredulous stares of the other drivers. I had an uncomfortable, nervous sensation that the car was about to explode or launch, maybe both. I pulled off the highway and into a service station. Fortunately there was a mechanic on duty.

After we described the strange behavior of the car, he looked askance at us, "The car is doing what?" he asked.

We repeated our explanation but it did not sound any more plausible the second time. Our laughter, as we recounted the incident, did not add credibility to our story. The mechanic's expression sent a clear message that he doubted our observations. As if to verify his suspicion, the car refused to repeat the errant behaviors.

After rummaging around, like mechanics do, for a brief few minutes, he announced authoritatively, "I do not see anything wrong."

Although we were near our destination, I did not want to be in an isolated spot in the dead of winter with a car that had God-knows-what wrong with it. I would have preferred the warmth of my own home. Since I was carrying a car phone, I called my friends at our destination to tell them we were turning back. They were concerned about the mechanical problems and offered to come get us, but I told them we were too apprehensive to go even farther from home. Whatever the problem, it seemed to have stopped for the moment.

The mechanic gave us a parting, "You girls take care now."

We pulled out of the service station and back onto the highway. We were traveling west this time, and headed back home. After about fifteen minutes my friend and I began to think differently about our decision. The longer we were distanced from the strange actions of the car, the more comfortable we became. Knowing little about mechanics, we assumed there must have been some self-correcting activity in the car's electrical system. (People with no mechanical ability think this way.) Since both of us really wanted to take this trip, and since we were still closer to that destination than to Portland, we decided to turn around and continue our trip. I again pulled off the highway, did a loop around and over a bridge, and headed east.

As soon as we had nosed the car back onto the highway, the strange activity of lights and locks began again. The strobe of lights and the noisy rhythm of the locks returned. The car was behaving as it saw fit without regard to the laws of its own mechanics. The irritation we might normally have felt with the automobile's mechanical problem was superseded by the eeriness of this unnatural occurrence. The uneasy feeling it created in my gut went beyond simple concern with the car's reliability to a greater concern about something more ominous.

We feared tempting the unknown any more and had to give in to the insistent gremlins of my minivan. We turned again for Portland. Once again, the car returned to performing as it had been designed to perform, smooth and quiet. We laughed uneasily at the way the car acted up, when we were headed toward our desired destination, and how it returned to normal as soon as we faced it home. It started to rain. It came down thick and heavy, the kind of rain one enjoys watching from the safe haven of home. The thermometer in the car registered freezing and was falling. The decision to return home appeared to be a wise one for, if we had continued, we might well have been stranded, or worse. Every once in a while my friend and I would fall silent, and I knew we both were wondering about any deeper meaning to our unusual trip. We arrived safely home without additional incident.

The following day I called my friends who we had tried to visit. The storm of the previous night had arrived earlier than had been expected. The roads had iced heavily, especially those passing up into the high desert where were going. The icy rain we had encountered on our return trip was the leading edge of a winter blast that had worsened throughout the night. We had been saved from a treacherous, perhaps dangerous journey. I knew we had been turned back from danger; we had not made the decision alone. Without our mysterious forces, we surely would have continued the journey and placed ourselves in harm's way.

I took my car in for service to the dealership the next day and told them to check out the electrical system. The car was still under warranty. I hoped that the warranty-certified mechanics might have better luck than the mechanic on the road. But I guess I was not totally surprised when they came back with the same answer, "nothing wrong." They were puzzled by my story, and assured me that the car would not be harmed if driven and that I should bring it back as soon as there was a recurrence of the electrical problem. It never recurred.

My friend and I had been journeying to meet with a number of Native American friends. The wise elder of this extended family, Buck Ghosthorse, has provided me and many others with instruction and wise counsel about the Red Road. I consider his residence to be one of my spiritual homes. The trips to and from are often meditative and reflective. On the way, I prepare myself for the enlightening lessons I will receive; as I return home, I process the teachings. On these travels the spirits' presence is often intensified, and I feel them evident as fellow passengers.

The termination of a trip there would normally have left me disappointed because of my lost learning opportunity. The wondrous nature of this particular adventure, however, left me far from disappointed. The spirits had not waited for me to seek them out. They had come unbidden in my time of need, even before I was aware there was a need. The gremlins in the automobile electrical system were truly my spiritual allies, providing loving protection. They were present, as always, as protectors and teachers.

This teaching provided me with the awareness that not only am I protected in non-ordinary reality during a journey, but this protection extends into the ordinary reality of life. I personally believe that when my spirit helpers said they were there to protect me, they meant it on all levels. It is my choice to believe in them wholeheartedly.

The Shamanic Journey

The shamanic journey is filled with mystery, and despite its ancient history, is little understood in Western culture. The journey is one of the most effective ways to make contact with the spirits. The altered state of consciousness achieved in a journey allows you to transcend the limitations of the rational world and connect with a non-ordinary reality. The shamanic journey is common to all cultures (even European) and the nature of the journey is remarkably similar, even in cultures widely separated by era and geography. In the spirit world, both time and place are illusions. The lessons from the other worlds are universally true, drawing from a collective consciousness that is accessible to all.

Learning how to journey successfully takes time and practice. The first step in journeying is stilling the mind, which often involves rhythmic drumming. Journeying requires you to tune in to all of your senses. It is vital to activate as many of the senses as possible to stimulate your powers of observation beyond the visual. Many people depend too much on the visual in journeying, and fail to access the total information contained in the journey. Often, the information will come through a sense of "knowingness," a kind of sixth sense that is beyond seeing or any of the other single senses.

To prepare for your journey by stimulating your senses, try this simple exercise:

Close your eyes and imagine a red rubber ball.
Bounce the ball and hear its bounce.
Throw the ball up against the wall.
Squeeze the ball; feel its texture.
Bring the ball up to your nose and smell it.
Stick your tongue out and taste it.

Now open your eyes. Could you see the ball? Could you hear the ball and notice the difference in sound qualities from bouncing the ball close to your feet and throwing it against a distant wall? Could you feel the elasticity of the ball and its texture? Could you smell it and taste it? Notice which of your senses was the strongest. If you close your eyes and it is totally black, then tune into your knowingness and "see" with that sense. Many people have absolutely no visual sense in a journey, yet the detail of the journey is exceptional.

This exercise will help you become more attuned to your senses and discover which ones are more vivid for you. The goal of the ball exercise is to literally activate your senses to a reality (the ball) that is not currently in your ordinary reality. In a journey, you will do the same thing. Through your senses you will activate a non-ordinary reality and journey through a place unfamiliar to your ordinary reality.

I have taught hundreds of people how to journey, many with remarkable success. However, I constantly hear from people that they could journey easily with me but struggled on their own. Often, after further discussion, I find that they do not take time to prepare before the journey. It is very important to still your mind and prepare your space anytime you choose to work with the spiritual realm. There is a sacredness to this activity that must be respected.

The Preparation for Journeying

The purpose of journeying is to connect with the spirit realm and to enter another reality from which to acquire greater understanding and awareness. Appropriate preparation requires attention to certain conditions. The following guidelines should enhance your journey experience:

1. *Declare a place of entry into the ground and do not change it.* This is a permanent place you will use each time you journey. This place will actually build a thought form of energy around it to reinforce the shamanic altered state of awareness. You will have consciousness of this thought form each time you approach the place, and your entry will be facilitated.

2. *Write the intention of your journey on a piece of paper.* Spend time getting the words just right. I have found that the clearer the intention, the clearer the journey will be.

3. *Prepare your space for journeying by cleansing the area.* I usually do this by burning white sage, but sometimes I use incense, essential oils, or bells. No one method is better than another, as long as the intention is good. Keep your intention focused on the fact that you are clearing away any type of negative energy and preparing yourself mentally.

4. *If you work with spirit helpers or wish to call in deities or other entities, this would be a good time to do so.* Filling the room with the energy of your communication with the spirits will enhance your journey.

5. *Sit or lie down and take time to relax your body.* Pay attention and tune in to what your own energy is doing. Take some deep breaths and start to relax.

6. *Open up the* chakras, which are energy centers in your body *in the following manner:*

    • Direct your thoughts to the *chakras* in your feet, which are major energy centers in the body and often forgotten. Open these *chakras* up simply by moving your intention to that area of your body and asking them to open. Ask the *chakras* to draw energy up from the ground—the earth—and to continue up your body, sending energy up through your legs and hips. When you reach the base of the spine, you are at the root *chakra*. Since the root *chakra* is located just above where you are sitting, or is against the ground if you are lying down, you can draw Earth's energy into this area. I like to cleanse the *chakras* before I put in new energy, so visualize the root *chakra* squeezing like a sponge to drain out the old energy and to fill with the new energy as it comes into your system.

    • There are colors commonly used for each of these *chakras*. You can enhance and activate the energy of each *chakra* if you think of its color—purge out the old stagnant color and refill with vibrant fresh color:

    —The first *chakra*, the root *chakra*, is red and is located at the base of your spine and down between your legs. Imagine the color red draining out of this area, like a sponge being squeezed until all the contents are removed. Then refill the base of your spine and root *chakra* with a strong, vibrant red color. Continue this process of purging and then refilling with energy through all of the *chakras*.

    —The second *chakra* is located in the abdominal area or the womb area; its color is orange. Again, visualize old orange color draining out of your abdominal area and then filling with vibrant orange color.

    —The third *chakra* is located in the solar plexus area and its color is yellow.

    —The fourth *chakra* is located in the heart area and its color is green.

    —The fifth *chakra* is located in the throat area and its color is blue.

—The sixth *chakra* is located in between the eyebrows, or the third eye area, and its color is indigo (a bright deep blue).

—The seventh *chakra* is located on the crown of the head and its color is violet or deep purple.

• I also like to run the energy down my shoulders, arms, hands, and out my fingers opening up the *chakras* in these areas. I can always feel my fingers start to tingle as the energy surges to this area. I use white for this area.

7. *Visualize your energy going out of your head and connecting to Spirit up above.* You should hold the feeling that you are connected to the heart of the earth, and through your own heart, to the heart of the universe. Visualize this energy circling back around from the universe and connecting to the earth. With this activity you have created a circle, a hoop, a medicine wheel of energy—from the earth through you to the universe and back around again. You notice that you are part of this circle, part of its energy. All is connected, whole, and complete, a continuous orbit of energy.

8. *Once you are connected, bring your focus to your breathing and your intention of entering into the spirit realm.* You are now prepared to begin your journey.

The Journey

Play a rhythmic drumming tape. Be sure the tape is sufficiently long to continue throughout the length of the journey, and that it is especially structured for journeying. An appropriate drumming tape will include a change in beat that marks a "call back." I use a drumming tape available from The Foundation for Shamanic Studies.

1. Lie down and take some deep breaths, filling yourself with power.

2. State your intention at least four times, in your mind or out loud.

3. Go to your place of entry into the earth and dive or jump in.

4. Count back from ten to one and feel yourself traveling through your entry. When you reach the number one, you declare yourself to be in the lower world.

5. Step out and call your power animal to you.

6. If this is your first journey and you do not have a power animal, call out a declaration that you are there to meet your power animal.

7. Watch which animals come into your awareness. If an animal shows itself four times, it has a high potential of being your power animal.

8. Ask it if it is your power animal and watch for a reply of some sort. Be sure to let the animal choose you, rather than you choosing it. It is important not to have a preconceived idea about your power animal.

9. Spend time interacting with your power animal. Feed and pet the animal, play with it, and start building a relationship. After you feel comfortable with your power animal, you may ask it your original intention four times.

10. If you know your power animal prior to entering the lower world, (showing itself four times is only for first-time journeyers), state your intention four times as soon as you meet it.

11. Begin your journey accompanied by your power animal.

12. When the drum beat changes to the call back, retrace your steps and replay the journey in your mind, setting it into your memory.

13. Return back up through your tunnel to your original place of entry.

After the Journey

After the journey is over, write it in your journal immediately. Recall as many details as you can, including feelings, colors, smells, textures, tastes, visual images, "knowings," and conversations. Remember that the images you bring back with you are largely metaphorical. It may take some time and guidance to understand their meanings. Frightening images are usually metaphors that may be projections of your own fears, but they are almost always there to teach you something.

Remember that your spirit helpers and power animals are magical and they can do anything. Birds can swim under water, whales can fly, and tigers can talk. They are your protectors and guardians. Ask them questions and always travel with them when you are in non-ordinary reality. They do not lie, that is only a human trait—you can trust them.

Each journey will be different; some will be more powerfully realized than others. You might want to journey first with an experienced guide until you have mastered the journey for yourself.

There is much to learn about the spiritual realm. In each journey I gather information concerning my intention, but I also listen openly for what the spirits may want to tell me. I have found the shamanic journey to be one of my most profound ways of connecting with the spirits and one of the richest sources of understanding and awareness.

To me, imagination is the gateway *into* the spiritual realm. It is not the spiritual realm, it is the way *in*. Imagination is a tool that we are given as children, but often forget how to use. Children usually have a profound awareness of the spiritual realm; they have wonderful vivid imaginations, and many have imaginary friends. Children become completely entranced with other realities; they easily talk to trees, sing to flowers, see magical kingdoms in sparkling sand, and physically "see" spirits. Kids see and communicate with spirit beings quite naturally.

Unfortunately, these fabulous imaginations are often stifled as children grow up and conform to society. Family, school, church, and other external forces of the culture shape their beliefs and responses. Mothers lovingly but with authority, say, "Now honey, you should not lie. There really is not anyone sitting next to you. Rocks do not have mouths and they cannot *really* talk." The fabulous, magical, fun, mystical connections are lost or blocked. What the spirits have taught me about imagination is that it is actually a gift from Spirit, and that Spirit is providing us with an avenue to creation and connection.

Imagination connects you back into the magical, mystical worlds of Spirit you once knew as a child. When I work with people in journeying they will often say, "I feel like I am making the whole thing up, like it is just my imagination."

And I say, "Good."

Imagination is the portal *in*. It gives permission to the psyche (your limited mind) to experience something that is out of the realm of what you would call an ordinary experience. Because of conditioning, you are extremely limited by your own perception of what you define as real. If the imagination can travel further into the realm of the unknown than your belief system allows, then by all means travel on the imagination. What you will find out is that you are not making it up at all. The spirits are alive and well, existing in other realities that you probably cannot see with your physical eyes, but are *real* just the same. The imagination provides the avenue to get there.

So use your imagination, develop it, and allow it to expand, create, grow, and become. Spirit continually provides you with ideas, information, possibilities, and potentials for your own growth and development.

Meditation

There are many methods of meditation, but all have the common goal of stilling the mind. A stilled mind is a focused mind. When you are able to focus your mind, you are in control of your thinking and your energy. Meditation enables this to happen.

Meditation connects you with your inner self and with Spirit. When you stop the commotion of the outside world, it is then possible to connect to your inner world. I often refer to this as "turning your outside ears off and turning your inside ears on."

Praying is talking to God, but meditation is *listening* to God. When you still the mind, you open yourself to receive information from non-ordinary sources. Information may come in diverse and unusual ways. You might see a series of colors, shapes, or symbols. You might hear distant sounds of the universe. You may receive sensations of knowingness or remembering. All of these are indicators of the opening of your nonlinear mind, of opening to the realm of Spirit. Through meditation, you consciously tune into your spirit form (remember you are a spirit having a human experience, not a human having a spiritual experience) and communication is different in that realm. It does not matter if you understand all the information or the symbols you receive, but it is important that you be receptive to the information. Spirit will provide the opportunities for you to learn. Trust that.

If nothing is happening for you, and you continually stay in the blackness of the *void*, that is wonderful, stay there. The void is the ultimate goal for many. Let that be.

A spiritual teacher of mine once said, "Never is nothing happening."

Meditation can be a great time of release, of allowing yourself to just relax and slip into nothingness. It can be a way of handing situations over and asking Spirit to take care of them. Also, meditation provides you the opportunity to journey deep within yourself and feel. The journey into self will be your most difficult and most rewarding journey. St. Augustine said, "The longest journey ever taken is from your head to your heart." Meditation connects you to your heart.

Meditation provides for an intimate love relationship with Spirit. It is gentle and passive, well worth the effort. Many people attempt to meditate and get frustrated in the process. It feels too difficult. The mind wanders. You cannot stay focused. You get frustrated and plug right into the underlying belief system that claims, "I've failed again."

In reality, most people set their goals too high when they begin meditating. Going into the void, which is a place of complete stillness, is very difficult because most people have never even attempted to still their minds or control their thoughts. In this culture we are not trained in how to still the mind. In fact, we over-stimulate it through television, computerized graphics, video games, and flashing neon lights. All this brightness and intense stimulation can be like jet fuel for the brain. To slow the mind after decades of this type of stimulation can be quite a challenge. My suggestion is to take baby steps so that you do not become discouraged.

A good first step in meditation is learning to concentrate. An excellent beginning tool is a guided meditation tape in which the narrator leads you through the process of relaxation and stilling the mind. Listening to the tape will teach you to focus on the words, and it will have a cumulative effect on your psyche. If you choose a tape that helps you with a current issue, you not only are learning how to focus your mind, you are also receiving both a conscious and subconscious healing. There are many good tapes on the market covering a wide variety of topics. Your intention should be to listen with great intensity and focus on every word.

When you feel you have mastered the tape and are having success with focusing on the words, shift your attention to the voice inflections. You might not even hear the words anymore, but you are now listening to tone quality. What does the voice sound like? Listen for the differences in tone, pitch, and volume. After you have mastered that, see if you can hear the breathing of the individual talking on the tape. Does it increase or decrease anywhere? What you are doing is focusing your mind through your listening. You are concentrating and actually selecting what you choose to focus on. You are getting control of your thoughts.

Once you have mastered the auditory form, try focusing your mind by looking at a picture and work on your visual sense. Look carefully at the picture, pulling out as many details as you can. Then close your eyes and see if you can remember the details. Do this over and over again until you can detail the whole scene in your mind. Then concentrate on the colors in the picture. Single out individual colors noticing the different shades and hues represented. Do this for each color in the picture. Then do shapes. You will find that your concentration and focusing abilities improve, as will your memory. These two abilities—concentration and memory—go hand in hand. The more you focus, the greater your memory will develop.

Next, try an activity with touching. Get an object, close your eyes, and learn to feel. Spend days working on texture, shape, and surface characteristics. Try replicating the object in your mind with your eyes closed. Feel it with each of your senses.

Once you feel your abilities of concentration are honed, you are ready to attempt meditation. Go back to auditory tapes, but this time listen to music that is trance inducing. Tibetan horns are very effective, as are chants. As you listen to the tape, pay attention to your breathing. Focus on every breath, the in and out motion of your stomach and chest, the feelings of filling and releasing, and the sounds and rhythms of your breath. Keep focused on your breathing as long as you can. If thoughts wander into your consciousness, allow them to slip gently by and bring your awareness back to your breathing. This rhythm of your relaxed breathing and the sound of the music induces a deep meditative state.

When you feel ready, try the meditation without music. Sit comfortably, close your eyes, and still the mind. You are ready to go into the place of complete stillness on your own—the void, the quiet mind. You will now be able to experience, as you float off to this incredible place called the void, the feelings of euphoria and divine peacefulness. This is how to connect to the divine self—to Spirit—unencumbered by your thoughts.

Even with all of this practice, do not set your goal too high. Start small and gradually increase the endurance of complete stillness. It will take several weeks to complete these exercises, but enhancing your focusing skills is worth the time invested. The ability to concentrate and focus will help you in every phase of life. You will notice a change in the stress you carry, in your tolerance of situations and others, and in your attitude toward life.

Preparing to Meditate

The preparation for meditation is nearly identical to that for journeying. (See **page 127** for details about preparation). The purpose of both practices is to connect with Spirit and to enter another reality. Both practices require cleansing of the space for sacred use, honoring the spirits, and keeping clear one's intention. The chakras play an important role in getting grounded for the experience. The chart below is a reminder of the colors of each chakra, which might be helpful in your visualization. Cleansing one's chakras prior to meditation can enhance the experience, just as it is good preparation for journeying. Once you have prepared your space, grounded yourself, cleansed your chakras, and declared your intention, bring your focus to your breathing and relax. Concentrate on quieting the mind and going into the void, that sublime state of stillness. This peace is the intention of meditation.

CHAKRA	COLOR
Root	Red
Abdominal/Womb	Orange
Solar Plexus	Yellow
Heart	Green
Throat	Blue
Third Eye (mid-brow)	Indigo
Crown	Violet

Conclusion

Life is a journey of becoming. The goal of the journey is not in its destination—rather, it is the understanding that emerges from the journey. It is through the journey that wisdom is gained.

Those who are interested in experiencing wisdom must change; they must seek healing. They must look at what they believe and examine why they believe it. The care of the soul can have magical results; soul retrievals and healings can be life altering. I have witnessed hundreds of healings. They were all miraculous, beautiful, loving, and real. I have also witnessed healings that did not last. Many people do not feel worthy to receive their healings. Spirit consistently provides opportunities to heal, but until you make the decision to change your life and to change your thinking, you will find a way to reject the healing.

Our society looks for quick fixes with minimal personal commitment. People schedule healings like they do hair appointments! They expect a new "do," and it becomes the practitioner's job to create it. Miracles can occur in an instant, but sustaining the miracles of life requires a personal commitment to change the faulty patterns that created the woundedness. It is a daily job, but one of joy.

Please take heed of these final words of advice for success along your spiritual path:

1. Let go of the people, places, and things that block you from your own growth.

2. Forgive.

3. Pray and pray and pray.

4. Develop a relationship with Spirit—journey, meditate, connect in some way, and trust the information that comes to you.

5. Take care of your soul. Contact people who can help you with this care.

6. Scrutinize your belief system. Is your core foundation based on fear or love?

7. Practice random acts of kindness and compassion.

8. Be humble and open.

9. Love yourself and all life (including rocks!).

10. Learn the laws of energy and practice them.

11. Put your energy into what you want to create for yourself. Do not worry!

12. Practice mantras and affirmations.

13. Look closely at yourself, your behaviors, and your beliefs, and then make conscious decisions about change.

14. Pay attention to what you attract to yourself. Understand how this attraction is linked to your electromagnetic field of energy. Determine which core belief is creating your magnetic charge.

15. Remember that you contribute to the collective consciousness with every thought you have. Are you contributing positive energy or reinforcing negativity?

16. Get clear as to what you would like to create for yourself. What do you ultimately desire? Visualize yourself living this reality.

17. Devise ways to remind yourself each day to keep on track with your new way of being.

18. Choose rituals and ceremonies to enhance your spiritual connection.

19. Get with like-minded people and start building a new community. Support each other and yourself.

20. Make a commitment.

21. Talk to the spirits and then "feel" their answer.

22. Love yourself!

We are in a new millennium. Change is upon us. The whole universe supports a new connection for those who choose it. People are seeking their divinity, their connection to Spirit and to God. We are in the transition to the Golden Age—the age in which souls are connected to Source, to God, to Spirit. Heavy veils are lifting.

Our culture historically has not endorsed the magic, the miracles of connection, and Spirit. We have spent hundreds of years out of touch with our own divinity. Many humans have spent lifetimes experiencing the hardships in life—betrayal, doubts, prejudice, abuse, unworthiness, inadequacy, hatred, and war. These lifetimes were not based in love but in fear. Even many who believed in God chose their belief through fear. Judgment, judgment, judgment controlled their behavior and their life. They were either afraid of being judged or they were judging themselves. Many sought connection through another being, someone who had more connection, more worth than they. But this is illusion. Worth is intrinsic, and connection is everyone's birthright. It is through your healing that the world will heal—that life will heal.

Remember the spirits *love you*; they want you to be happy and fulfilled. Desire the same for yourself, for happiness is a choice.

Many years ago I wrote the following letter to a pastor of the church I was attending with my family.

Dear Jim:

Ever since your sermon on Sunday, I've been thinking of what you said concerning happiness and if anyone was willing to share stories. I am, and mine is pretty simple. There was no big event that pried open my eyes, but an awareness that developed from a personal journey searching for happiness.

It all started with the question: Happiness, what is it? I wasn't sure, but I knew it could feel better than my present state of being. I proceeded to pray and concentrate with God about happiness. I would look at my world and see such beautiful things. A wonderful husband and family, great friends, excellent health, super living conditions. I would actually have pangs of guilt. Why wasn't I truly happy? What needed to happen? Who needed to come into my life? What was the formula? What was I suppose to do? What was the correct prayer? What was blocking me? I was determined to answer these questions. Being the studious type, I looked for readings and other sources of ideas. If looking to learn, I must study. There must be a method, a procedure to follow in order to gain true happiness. I started exploring my character and myself. I must be flawed. I analyzed the situations, the people that molded me into what I am. Who harmed me in my childhood? What past event robbed me of my happiness? I was trying to explain and understand, searching through hidden memories, secrets of the past, and explanations of treatments. All of this opened many doors; self-actualization and awareness became part of me, but what of the happiness I still desired? Why was it still missing? What else could I study? What else could I learn? Who could show me the way?

Then the day came when I truly understood. No particular external event took place, but an amazing internal transformation of thought occurred. I had read many philosophies about happiness, but it was when I decided to become happy that the transformation developed. The answer to happiness was not only before me, it was me. An acceptance of who I am, how I relate to the world, and what my role is in life. Happiness, true happiness is an attitude: An acceptance of self. It took me twelve years of searching for the external blessings that hid the internal truths. The truth was my thoughts. I gained sight by listening to my thoughts, what I said to myself in that constant self-talk that we all experience. It was all in my head, that internal world of thought, my experiences, my past, my God, all interrelating. I gained an understanding of it all working together; the right formula, the right method, the right path, and I listened to my heart to know who I am. Then, I was there. I had achieved my quest—a personal achievement of being satisfied with myself and accepting others as themselves. I understood that complete happiness does not mean being immune to the hardships of life, but is about the attitude that springs from those hardships. Happiness is a choice, a simple conclusion of thought. Change your thoughts and you change your feeling. A concept so simple but made so complicated. I robbed myself of what God automatically had given me as one of his children. God has the answers, the methods, the paths well marked for those who request the journey. It will be different and personal for all, but the outcomes will be the same. Happiness, peace, harmony and love.

Always a choice,

Jan Engels-Smith

Know yourself, honor yourself, take care of yourself, become yourself.

Other work by Jan Engels-Smith

Take Your Body with You. A shamanic drumming CD. This amazing CD was produced by Jan and five other people. It is channeled. This CD is exceptional in creating the atmosphere, rhythm, and frequencies of vibration to reach an altered state of consciousness and contact with non-ordinary reality.

Journeying is the foundational tool for shamanic study and healing. It provides the passageway that has been used for centuries to obtain information from other dimensions, realms, and realities. Through the journeying process, you can connect with your power animals and spiritual teachers. Information, knowledge and wisdom becomes available to you that you can utilize for solving problems, gaining clarity about life's circumstances or simply to build your awareness and understanding of the different worlds beyond. Journeying is a perfect way to learn what needs to unfold in your life and then actively integrate this information to help you maximize your happiness and wholeness.

Journeying is typically taught by lying down, covering your eyes and listening to a drumming CD. This is a great way to journey; however, many indigenous shamans ***took their bodies with them***. Shamans journeyed while dancing and singing using their body as a vehicle to contact spirit. As you listen to this CD, experiment, move your body, slightly close your eyes, sing if you like, and see what happens.

Jan has included a "calling to the spirits" sequence at the beginning. This is done through whistling and songs that invoke spirits to assist you during your journey process.

Jan's personal philosophy is to assist individuals in gaining their own personal empowerment that in turn promotes self-healing, better communities, and a healthier world. She believes that each soul is exquisite in nature, that it is radiant, brilliant and magnificent. Jan believes that discovering this innate truth about yourself is a major step in creating a balanced world. She believes that the world is a reflection of your own perception and when your perception of yourself changes, the world reflects that back to you.

This CD was channeled. Jan has never heard this beat before nor has she been able to duplicate it again. The sounds and voices are of a tribe that came through the participants to spread their message of healing through sound and vibration. Her teaching from these spirits has been that all things are made of energy: sound, light, and frequencies of vibration and that certain vibrations heal and move energies in a healing way. Also vibrations create portals into different realities for us to explore and from which to bring back useful information. This CD is a product of these teachings.

To order a CD or to obtain information about Jan's classes and workshops, please contact her:

Jan Engels-Smith
LightSong Healing Center
LightSong School of Shamanic Studies
www.janengelssmith.com

Bibliography

Course in Miracles. Glen Ellen, California:
   Published by the Foundation for Inner Peace,1975

Eakins, Pamela. *Tarot of the Spirit.* York Beach, Maine:
   Samuel Weiser, Inc.1992

Haich, Elizabeth. *Initiation.* London England:
   Unwin Hyman Limited,1965

Harner, Michael. *The Way of the Shaman.* 3rd edition, San Francisco, California:
   Harper and Row,1990

Ingerman, Sandra. *Soul Retrieval: Mending the Fragmented Self.* New York, New
   York.
   Harper Collins,1991

0-595-32474-6

Printed in the United States
25809LVS00006B/178-195

9 780595 324743